F L.3S

THE ARCHAEOLOGY
OF WETLANDS

John Coles
Professor of European Prehistory
University of Cambridge

D1610610

EDINBURGH
at the University Press

© John Coles 1984
Edinburgh University Press
22 George Square, Edinburgh
Set in Linoterm Times by
Speedspools, Edinburgh and
printed by Alna Press Ltd
Scotland

British Library Cataloguing
in Publication Data
Coles, John
The archaeology of wetlands.
1. Archaeology—Methodology
2. Wetlands
I. Title
930′.09′60   CC77.w4

ISBN 0 85224 489 4 (Hardback)
ISBN 0 85224 503 3 (Paperback)

Preface

The idea for this book originated many years ago in the peatbogs of the Somerset Levels, and it has developed through fieldwork and travels to other wetland regions in Europe and America. Beneath the fragile surface of the world's wetlands, whether they be marsh or lake, peatbog or swamp, are to be found not only unique and exciting ancient artifacts but also a variety of wetland archaeologists, digging, pumping, diving and unscrambling the tangled remains of prehistoric and historic occupations. Through contact with these wetlanders, I have learned much, and I hope that some of the information about wetland archaeology which I have attempted to advance here will meet with their approval. I owe particular thanks to those who have sent illustrations and information for this book; the brief mention of names, and notes in text or captions, are no real acknowledgement of their usefulness. And I have benefited greatly from regular discussions about wetland archaeology with David Hall (Fenland) and Bryony Orme (Somerset Levels) in the course of collaborative work in these areas.

JOHN COLES
Fitzwilliam College
Cambridge
1 February 1984

1

First Principles

INTRODUCTION. Wetland archaeology is a term not often encountered in textbooks dealing with either the history of archaeology or the
techniques used by archaeologists. Wetlands as an environment do not
regularly figure in the minds of archaeologists, who generally concern
themselves with such standard types of evidence as postholes, rubbish
pits, charcoal patches, stone tools, metal artifacts and potsherds. All of
these features occur on dryland archaeological sites, and our minds are
therefore conditioned to think that such evidence is traditional and fully
rewarding, and that in order to reconstruct patterns of human behaviour
we can and need obtain nothing more than this type of evidence.

All archaeological evidence is incomplete, and anything we can get
that adds to the record is valuable, especially if it opens a new vista, or
creates a new dimension, for our imperfect view of the past. The
concept of wetland archaeology is extremely simple: a wetland environment, and there are many of these, will add greatly to our
knowledge and understanding of past human behaviour, through the
effect of preservation of the evidence. Evidence that has perished on
dryland sites may be preserved on wetland sites, and to neglect this
source is to ignore a potentially and demonstrably fruitful area of
enquiry which can add much to our ideas about the past.

It is the aim of this book to present some thoughts on the value of
wetland archaeology as well as to describe some of its techniques and
discoveries.

DEFINITIONS. A wetland is any area of land covered by water for part
of each year, or of each day, or which has been drowned by water at
any time in its existence. Seasonal or climatic factors are important,
and a range of environmental conditions creates the possibilities for
wetlands. In formal terms, there are four major wetland types, i)
ponds or lakes; ii) marshes; iii) swamps; and iv) peatbogs. But
ancient man did not always live in or beside such damp conditions and

1

so, for archaeology, a further type of environment is important, where v) a former dryland has been overwhelmed by water (rising lake or river waters, development of peat, or other factors). In these five conditions, the vital element is water, sufficient to waterlog the immediate environment and thus prevent decay of organic material. For the purposes of this book, I exclude underwater archaeology as it is practised on shipwreck sites; for this demands a separate treatment, as can be seen from recent studies (e.g. Muckelroy 1978).

i) *Ponds and lakes* form in well-defined basins, with either regular or uneven inflows and outflows of water; parts may dry out during drought or other conditions of low water levels. Ancient communities often established their settlements or carried out other activities on the shores and edges of such bodies of water (figure 1a). Material thrown into the water, or submerged by rising waters and then covered by silts and muds, may become waterlogged and thus preserved in good condition. However, this is not always the case, for subsequent drying-out may reduce the ancient sites to the equivalent of ordinary dryland occupations where preservation is not particularly good. Yet the mere act of sealing occupation levels by silts or muds can preserve quite remarkable evidence about past activities; the multiple horizons of occupation at Neolithic and Bronze Age sites in the Alpine lakes, representing ancient occupations sealed by rising water, are without doubt the best examples of this phenomenon (Ruoff 1981a). Some of these sites are noted in this book.

ii) *Marshes* tend to be flooded periodically, by seasonal climatic conditions, and the water levels fluctuate widely (figure 1b). During dry seasons, grasses may flourish and attract animals, including man; during some wet periods in the year, reeds, sedges and rushes will grow, and conditions may permit the protection and partial preservation of ancient remains. Such remains are not likely to be those encountered on sites based upon firmer drier land, so that the specialised nature of marshland occupation can seldom be used as a guide to the practices carried out in other landscapes. For example, the marsh-dwellers of the Tigris-Euphrates region today live and work in an extreme environment dominated by water, and all of their material possessions and activities reflect this (Thesiger 1964). Marshes in northern latitudes are not so hospitable, and during cold and wet seasons, major flooding may range across the marsh, causing many

2

plants to perish, and animal activities dependent upon the plants to cease.

iii) *Swamps* are a better environment as archaeological wetland; a swamp is in essence a wooded marsh where water may remain ponded or flow gently through the year (figure 1c). Trees such as willow or alder, or even birch, will grow in drier clumps in European swamps or carrs, and in America, blackgum, white cedar and larch will flourish. Swamps are fertile areas, and they were often selected by man for hunting and gathering practices, and indeed for clearance and cultivation if the excess water could be drained or eliminated. Many important, and often unusual, archaeological features have been noted in such wetlands; hunting stations and specialised platforms for burials are perhaps the most interesting. The Mesolithic station at Star Carr, Yorkshire, remains one of the most important wetland sites in Britain through its yield of organic evidence which threw new light upon early post-glacial activities (Clark 1954).

Not every traveller has been impressed by wetland environments such as swamp and marsh. In the nineteenth century, one marshland was unflatteringly described as 'either a gloomy waste of waters, or still more hideous expanse of reeds and other aquatic plants, impassable by human foot, and involved in an atmosphere pregnant with pestilence and death' (Warner 1826). On the other hand, an opposite view could be taken, and a contemporary swamp could be magnified into a land where 'aquatic flowers, of every variety and hue, are to be seen on every side, in pleasant contrast with the pale green of the sawgrass' (Smith 1847, for the Everglades of Florida). Both would agree on 'the profound and wild solitude of the place, the silence that pervades it' (*ibid.*), and it was this feature that helped in the selection of locations for monastic and other establishments in historic times in Britain and elsewhere. Athelney Abbey, founded in 878 AD, was 'so inaccessible on account of bogs and inundation of lakes that it cannot be approached but by a boat' (William of Malmesbury, quoted in Williams 1970).

iv) *Peatbogs* will form in almost any poorly-drained area where water accumulates and particular plants such as reeds, cotton grass and mosses flourish (figure 1d). The plants slowly decompose, layer by layer, to form peat, which is entirely organic (Godwin 1981). In a marsh, where the water lies throughout all or most of the year, the

3

Figure 1. a) A former lake-bay at Lough Gur, Ireland, gradually turning into a marsh as wetland plants encroach the margins and form a relatively stable base for plants of drier character. Communities c. 2000 BC lived beside the lake; b) View of seasonal floodwaters across part of the Somerset Levels, England. (Photo Bryony Orme.)

c) *A reed swamp in the Wye Valley, Ontario, Canada, where reeds and sedges flourish amidst the ponded and slow-moving waters; d) A fossil raised bog in the Somerset Levels, England; the bog has been partly cut for peat but allowed to flood, and cotton grass, moss and rushes have colonised, along with small birch and alder trees.*

Figure 2. A wooden trackway of c. 640 BC (XXI Le) in raised bog peats of Lower Saxony, Germany. Most of the pieces are split roundwood, with heavy longitudinals at the sides. (Photo H. Hayen.)

great reed *Phragmites* will flourish and through its annual cycles there will form layers of loosely-textured peat which may in time permit the growth of fenland shrubs and trees. Where drainage is poor, and rainfall high, raised bog may form on a relatively flat landscape, with *Sphagnum* moss as a dominant plant, although cotton grass and heather may also occur. The growth of these plants in conditions of poor drainage and high rainfall may create a domed bog, perhaps 10 m thick, holding vast quantities of acidic water. Ancient man never carried out traditional agricultural activities in raised bog areas, because of their acidity and wetness, but there are many accounts of other human activities in such bogs, including the construction of stone

6

and wooden trackways for crossing over the wetland (figure 2); these structures, and occasionally the wheeled vehicles used on some of them, present new kinds of evidence for archaeologists (Hayen 1983). Other archaeological discoveries in small bogs of northern Europe include the well-preserved remains of Iron Age people put to death and dumped in watery locations (Glob 1969).

Because raised bogs hold vast quantities of water, they act as giant sponges, and there are early accounts from Ireland and other areas which describe graphically the effects of bogflows, where the weight of water bursts the edge of the bog, and a mass of sodden peat and vegetation flows inexorably outwards, encompassing fields, cottages and all who are unable to escape (Kinahan 1897). A tantalising account of a wooden shed with stone axes and other artifacts lying about, totally buried by peat, may represent just such a hasty abandonment, as the survival of such a structure is otherwise unlikely (Mudge 1836).

Blanket bogland is another type of peatbog, where the drainage of water on hills and mountain slopes has been impeded by leaching and ironpan formation, so that the original dry surface is overwhelmed by the formation of a peat composed of such typical plants such as moss and heather (Hammond 1981). Blanket bogs have often obscured and protected ancient occupation surfaces on hills, although the extreme acidity is destructive of organic materials, and it is debatable whether they should be considered as true wetlands. Nonetheless, if we are concerned with the survival of evidence, then blanket bogs do indeed preserve ancient landscapes which would otherwise have been disturbed if not entirely destroyed by subsequent occupations. The discovery in blanket bog in Ireland of hill and valley systems of field walls and banks, with the land divided into Neolithic fields, and settlements and burial places predictably positioned, opens up new possibilities for archaeological survey, excavation and interpretation (Caulfield 1983); for it is rare to find more or less intact prehistoric landscapes where the movements of people within their own land tenure can be documented with precision.

These general definitions of wetlands do not exhaust all the varieties, and the terms used in different parts of the world to describe wetlands are not consistent. *Fenland* is a case in point (Godwin 1978); here sedges are dominant, *Sphagnum* moss is rare, and the acid environment is less marked. Reeds, shrubs and occasional trees may flourish in a fen (figure 3). *Muskeg* is a North American term for a vast expanse of wetland which approaches a fen in parts, but is often more acidic, although equally boggy – 'his mind is a muskeg of mediocrity' (J. Macnaughton 1858–43). The environmental history of a wetland such as the English Fens is very complex. The influence of sea-level change was great in creating widespread periods of flooding which led to the deposition of silts and clays, and to the formation of peats. A popular term for wet acidic environments is *bogland,* but this is only a general and very unspecific definition which covers a variety of different circumstances. The great bogoaks recovered from many peat deposits indicate as clearly as any other sign that environmental conditions in such wetlands were variable and not always aquatic.

Peatbogs cover about 2 million hectares of the world, and, of this enormous area, more than 95% is in northern latitudes, and 80% lies in vast tracts of Russia and America. However, there are huge areas of general peatlands in other northern regions such as Finland, Sweden and Ireland (Griffin 1982).

Wetlands are not unimportant today. If active, they collect and filter rain and snow, they maintain water tables, they house countless plants and animals, and until recently they were not particularly attractive to humans for 'development'. Wetlands cover about 6% of the total land area of the world, and are part of the original natural environment; yet more than desert, savannah or even jungle, wetlands are today the most threatened of all land types. By their nature they tend to be fertile, particularly if the acidity can be reduced. Marshes and swamps are often base-rich, and their muds and decayed vegetation permit cultivation or, more often, the establishment of grassland grazing. Drainage of these is simple, and peatbogs when perforated or channelled can also be dried-out rapidly. The mixing of base-rich soils with acidic peat can create a fertile environment for grasses or other plants, and many wetlands of all types are today being turned to grassland or arable. Where this is not possible, or not required, then some wetland peats can be quarried for fertilisers, or burnt for electricity generation.

There are many agencies concerned about such fundamental alterations to human environments, and archaeologists should ally themselves with such conservation interests. Not to do so is to allow the destruction of just those archaeological sites which could bring new

8

Figure 3. A developing fen, with alder colonising a wet surface dominated by sedge tussocks ('elephant grass'); hazel and oak demonstrate that firmer (drier) conditions exist in parts of the area. (Photo B. J. Orme.)

evidence to bear on our studies of past human behaviour. Such new evidence is unmatched on any other type of site, except those under the extreme aridity of north African or other sands, or those frozen by the extreme cold of central Asia or the Arctic.

WETLANDS AND ARCHAEOLOGY. Wetlands, of whatever sort, have a unique quality, the ability to preserve a wide range of material by the creation of anaerobic conditions. The great volume of water contained within wet silts, muds, and peats prevents or hinders biological decay, and ancient artifacts incorporated in these deposits can be preserved intact or only slightly deteriorated. A brief consideration of several sites will show why this is important for archaeology, and this will be prefaced by a general comment on the nature of archaeological evidence.

Since the start of archaeological discovery and excavation, the materials recovered have been overwhelmingly of *inorganic* composition. Flint and stone; gold, copper, bronze, and iron; and baked clay, form the bulk of artifacts excavated from the burial mounds, camps, tells and caves of prehistoric Europe, Asia and America. Animal bones were often the only organic elements noticed on some of these sites. And the sites themselves generally consisted of heaps or scatters of earth or stone, ditches and pits, postholes and hearths, representing the decayed state of former structures. For Europe at least, it was logical to try to arrange the artifacts in terms of their materials, and to base a chronology on the Three Age system: Stone, Bronze, Iron. Yet when anthropologists and explorers ventured into less-developed parts of the world they recorded that almost every community they encountered had basically relied on organic materials for shelter, tools, weapons, ornaments, and food. Inorganic substances, though important and valuable, formed only a small proportion of the total range of artifacts, and were often used to make primary tools (axes, knives) which then served to help manufacture the objects actually used in day-to-day existence. Stone and metal tools were used to shape the house posts, digging sticks, bows, bowls and other equipment actually used in daily life by the communities. Whereas the primary inorganic artifacts might well be rather generalised in shape, the secondary, organic, objects allowed humans to exercise their imagination and to develop traditional shapes and styles, unique to each particular society. For archaeologists interested in identifying aspects of past human behaviour, an interpretation based on both organic and inorganic evidence must be far more reliable than one based only on primary inorganic components.

The Table attempts to show the varieties of material preserved on

10

TABLE 1. The *preservation* of materials on sites

	Dryland	Wetland
Imperishables	80-100%	10-25%
stone	++	++
flint	++	++
bronze	+/++	++
glass	+/++	+/++
pottery	++/--	+/++
shell	+/--	+
bone	++/--	++/--
antler/horn	+/--	+/-
iron	+/--	++/-
shale	+/-	++/+
carbonised plants	+/-	+
wood	-/--	++/+
plants	-/--	++/+
leather/hide	--	++/-
textiles	--	+/-
basketry	--	+/-
invertebrates	-/--	+
Perishables	0-20%	75-90%

Examples:

Mesolithic	Morton (Scot)	Tybrind Vig (Den)
Neolithic	Elsloo (Neth)	Charavines (Fr)
	Hambledon (Eng)	Alvastra (Swed)
Bronze Age	Postoloprty (Czech)	Auvernier (Switz)
	Itford Hill (Eng)	Fiavè (Italy)
Iron Age	Heuneburg (Germ)	Glastonbury (Eng)
Early historic	Vorbasse (Den)	Feddersen Wierde (Germ)
	Chalton (Eng)	Novgorod (USSR)

Symbols: ++ well preserved; + partly preserved, may be decayed; − poorly preserved, badly decayed; −− not preserved.
Note: Not all materials would have been present on all the sites noted (e.g. no glass on Mesolithic sites!), and conditions and therefore preservation are rarely standard throughout an entire site.

dryland and wetland sites, with examples of archaeological sites in Europe. The materials or artifacts are listed in descending order of 'perishability', with stone and flint at one end, and fragile basketry and invertebrate animal remains at the other (cf. figure 4). The material recovered from a dryland site, that is a site now dried out completely

11

with almost all organic remains disintegrated and lost, will often consist of 80–100% inorganic remains, some bone perhaps, and maybe shell and antler, but no wood or hide. Accepting the ethnographic evidence for the widespread use of wood for all manner of artifacts, dryland sites are certainly biased towards the inorganic components.

By contrast, a wetland site may contain a very wide range of materials, including stone and flint, right through the list to the most fragile textiles and basketry (figure 5), invertebrate remains and plant seeds and leaves. Detailed examination confirms that often only 10–25% of the total range of evidence will be based on inorganic components, with 75–90% being of organic origin. Indeed, some sites will be entirely organic, and without wetland preservation they would be lost completely, leaving no trace whatsoever. The upper parts of drying peats in Somerset, for example, contain wooden structures such as trackways or platforms once waterlogged and intact but now partly desiccated, with their surfaces disintegrating and active biological activity likely to lead to almost total loss in only a few years (Coles and Orme 1980). As such structures were made entirely of wood, their loss will completely remove part of the human record of activity in this area. As another example, fishing by use of wooden weirs and elaborate basketry funnels was a well established technique in many periods, yet through decay we have hitherto had very little information about this industry. Sections and fragments of fish weirs from many wetland sites now demonstrate the variety of methods used, and the unusual character of the evidence available for study (figure 6); these sites span over 5000 years, from Tybrind Vig, Denmark (c. 4000 BC) and Boylston Street, Boston (c. 2000 BC), to Sapporo on Hokkaido, Japan, the River Trent in England, and Little Qualicum River, British Columbia (c. 1000 AD), to more recent examples from e.g. Wapoto Creek, Washington (c. 1500 AD) (Andersen 1980; Johnson 1949; Salisbury 1981; Bernick 1983; Munsell 1976).

Settlements built in wet locations, or which became covered by waterlogged deposits, may be preserved in part so that in many cases the individual houses can be identified by still-standing lower parts of walls (Pétrequin 1983), or internal partitions, and of course a wide range of organic and inorganic debris may remain *in situ*. The settlement of Feddersen Wierde, for example (figure 7) is of fundamental importance to our understanding of the first millennium AD in

12

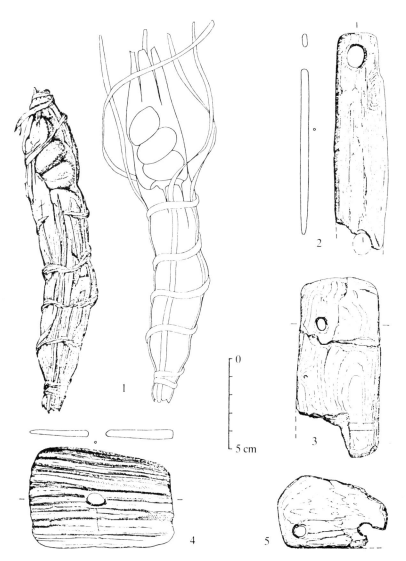

Figure 4. Fishing equipment from the Neolithic settlement of Twann, Switzerland, and examples of the extreme ranges of perishable/imperishable materials. 1 net sinker of pebbles wrapped and tied with bark; 2-5 bark floats. On a dry site, only about 10 unmodified pebbles would remain. (From Pétrequin 1984.)

13

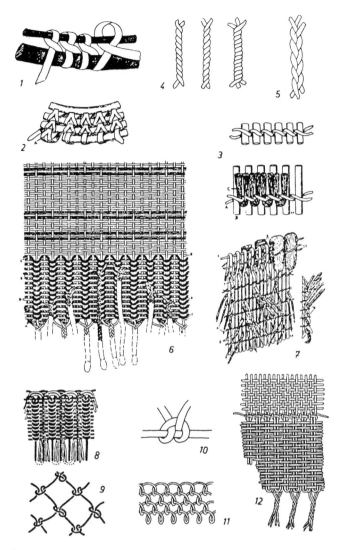

Figure 5. Basketry and textiles from Neolithic settlements in the Alpine lakes. 1-3 woven basketry details; 4-5 two- and three-strand cordage; 6 flax (linen) textile with cord fringe; 7-8 details of textiles and weaving; 9-11 netting; 10 knot; 12 linen with reinforced border. (From Pétrequin 1984.)

14

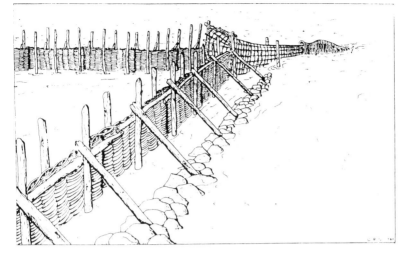

Figure 6. Reconstruction drawing of an Anglo-Saxon weir in Nottinghamshire, England, showing the woven panels, stake uprights and stone weights. (From Salisbury 1981.)

northern Germany (Haarnagel 1979); had it dried out before archaeological investigation, our understanding of the structure of the occupations, the identification of workshops for leather, wood, antler and bone, stalling for livestock, internal partitions within houses (cf. figure 8), and many other facets of life in the first two centuries A D, would be sadly reduced. The site would be no more than a rather ordinary although large native settlement. The same could perhaps be said for the broadly contemporary Elisenhof and Bosau settlements, where conditions were not as good for preservation, but where more recent excavation techniques could be used (Bantelmann 1975), so that much more environmental evidence was retrieved for analysis (Behre 1976; Hinz 1980).

Perhaps the best example is the information we now have from the Ozette Indian settlement on the Pacific coast, in Washington State, U S A. The site was near the base of an unstable hill slope, and about 500 years ago an underground stream swollen by seasonal waters suddenly created an enormous mudslide which buried part of the Indian settlement, including several houses and all of the equipment within and around them. The site was thus sealed, and subsequent mudslides preserved other later occupations. The methods of excavation of this

15

Figure 7. Feddersen Wierde, Germany, a settlement of the early centuries AD, to show the excellent preservation of house structures, internal partitions and fencing. (From Haarnagel 1979.)

Figure 8. Sketches of various walling retrieved from wet sites in Germany, Switzerland and Poland: 1 wattle-work, Ehrenstein, Germany; 2 stake foundation set in drilled planking, Aichbühl, Germany; 3 tied vertical stakes for flexible walling, Ehrenstein; 4 horizontal planks held by internal and external posts and stakes, Ehrenstein; 5 vertical plank wall, Niederwil, Switzerland; 6 lapped planking, Aichbühl; 7 planking tied by fibre, Aichbühl; 8 heavy horizontal plank wall slotted in posts, Biskupin, Poland. (From Pétrequin 1983.)

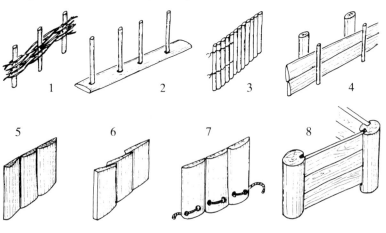

16

site are discussed below, but here we might point to the recovery of parts of the plank-built houses with adzed and carved panels (wolf and thunderbird designs), the main support posts for a roof, and abundant evidence of woodworking, basketry, weaving, fishing, whaling, sealing and artistry on a variety of materials (Gleeson and Grosso 1978). A harpoon whaling point, made of a sharpened mussel shell with antler barbs and string binding, kept in a cedar bark sheath, may demonstrate the unusual nature of the preservation, as does the recovery of over 18000 artifacts of plant material, mostly of woods such as red cedar, yew, fir and spruce.

A wetland site has the potential for a greater variety and abundance of evidence than does a dryland one, and it is a question not only of quality and quantity, but of the balance of evidence and evenness of the record. However, wetland sites are very uneven in their preservative characters, and an acidic peatbog may well destroy iron and even pottery while preserving wood, or it may be severe on bone and yet protect delicate seeds and leaves. The bog bodies from the Danish and north German peatbogs have clothing, skin, teeth and hair well-preserved, but their bones are often badly decayed (Glob 1969). The wooden pathways of north Germany have wooden components completely preserved, but bone artifacts are again poorly represented (Hayen 1980). Yet the Iron Age occupations of Somerset, taking place upon raised bogs in part at least, have been notable for excellent preservation of bone as well as wood (Bulleid and Gray 1911, 1917). And the lake-edge settlements of Switzerland, Italy and France are pre-eminent for the preservation of wood and most materials (figure 9), although inevitably it seems, textiles are among the most susceptible to deterioration (Keller 1878; Bocquet 1982; Ruoff 1981).

Other traces of human activities can survive in wetland locations, and may provide quite unusual evidence. Among these we might single out residues of plant and animal origin preserved in pottery or wooden vessels (e.g. Tybrind Vig, Denmark, Andersen 1980), or on the edges and surfaces of stone implements (e.g. the Sweet Track, England, Morris 1984). The recognition of blood residues on a selection of stone tools from prehistoric sites in British Columbia has allowed the identification of the animals cut by such tools, including caribou, moose, grizzly bear, sea lion and human (Loy 1983); any cleaning of the artifacts is likely to remove a large proportion of the residues, and a

17

wet – therefore protected – site, is more likely to preserve such residues than a dry or eroded one.

Although there is clearly considerable variation in wetland conditions for preservation, any reasonably wet environment has a unique advantage over dry conditions in terms of the likely existence of a greater range of evidence for the archaeologist.

Figure 9. Detail of vertical piles from one of the Fiavè settlements, Italy (Fiavè 6, c. 1350 BC). The substantial horizontal paired logs, held against the piles by short transverse pieces, created a firm structural base for the erection of houses upon platforms held above the wetland deposits. (Photo R. Perini.)

18

Figure 10. The first underwater excavation, 24 August 1854. Dr Adolphe von Morlot is shown on the bottom of the lake of Geneva, armed with a net and pick. (Drawn by A. von Morlot.)

History of research. The recognition of this fact, and the beginning of wetland archaeology, took place in 1854. It was well known that the shores of Lake Bienne in Switzerland had yielded remnants of wooden piles or posts, stuck in the lake muds, and associated with potsherds, stone axes, wooden tools and fragments of textiles, but these discoveries had not been accompanied by archaeological investigations of a systematic kind. In the winter of 1853–4, a severely-lowered water level on Lake Zurich revealed wooden posts lining areas of the lakebed just off the present shore, and Ferdinand Keller, President of the Antiquarian Society of Zurich, identified these as the remains of pile-dwellings of the Neolithic and Bronze Age (Martin-Kilcher 1979). The first archaeological excavation, if it can be so described, took place in 1854 when Adolphe Morlot, a geologist from Bern, descended a ladder from a boat in the waters of the Lake of Geneva, and, with a glass-fronted bucket on his head, an air tube, a pick and butterfly net, he gathered a range of ancient relics from the lakebed (figure 10). He stated, 'It was strikingly poetical to stand amid those ancient posts in the bluish twilight' (Speck 1981). A few of the niceties of modern wetland and underwater excavations may have been

19

missing from this first encounter, but interest in the potential of such wet sites was aroused, and Keller's regular reports in the decades following listed the work of wetland archaeologists in the lake muds of Germany, France and Italy. By 1870 the full recognition of the unusual, almost unique, character of such sites was established, and specialists in faunal and floral analyses were engaged (Keller 1878). The nineteenth-century excavations in the lake settlements yielded remains of platforms, causeways and palisades, dugouts, a huge array of small artifacts of stone, flint, bronze, pottery, wood and textiles, abundant food remains of wild and cultivated plants, and animal bones. Work of a more modern kind, with a full complement of environmental and economic analyses, is now in progress on many of these lakeside settlements, and some of the techniques are noted elsewhere in this book. The achievement of the pioneers lies not in their interpretations of the sites, as these have been dramatically modified in recent years, but in their recognition and persistence of belief in the outstanding interest and quality of wetland sites, sites which still astound archaeologists of a dryland upbringing.

The publication in the late nineteenth century of the results of the early Swiss work led a number of antiquaries to search for comparable wetland sites in other parts of the world. In Florida, the anthropologist Frank Cushing discovered, and excavated in the muck (peat with some inorganic component) at Key Marco, a late prehistoric (AD 1400–1500) settlement, which had been wrecked, perhaps by a hurricane, and its collapsed debris incorporated in a marsh. Cushing recovered and published a vast array of wooden artifacts carved by Calusa Indian craftsmen (Cushing 1897); his excavations yielded 11 barrels and 57 crates of perishable materials, some of which were conserved for study. It is unfortunate that to this day no other site has been identified in the area which contains such a range of organic materials, and the mere listing of these from Key Marco cannot demonstrate the details of carving, and the artistry, commemorated by the artifacts and which would otherwise be totally unknown (Gilliland 1975).

Common wooden artifacts from Key Marco, mostly of pine and cypress, include bowls, mortars and pestles, dumbbell pounders, boxes, trays, hafts and handles (with shell, bone and sharks' teeth blades), pins, paddles, atlatl handles and darts, toys (including catamaran canoe), peg floats with fishing nets and shell and stone weights.

20

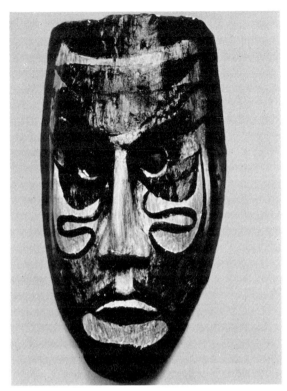

Figure 11. A wooden mask made by Calusa Indians of southern Florida, USA, retrieved by Frank Cushing in his pioneering excavations at Key Marco in the late 19th century. (Restored. Photo G. Macdonald and B. Purdy.)

Unusual wooden artifacts include carved human masks (some with shell-insert eyes, others painted) (figure 11), animal masks (including alligator head), plaques or standards (either flat planks, including one with painted woodpecker design, or carved with feline designs), a carved and painted deer head with ears pegged to fit, a carved kneeling feline figure, and a four-legged stool (probably used by the Calusa chief according to Spanish records of the first encounters between Europeans and Calusa Indians).

At the same time as Cushing worked at Key Marco, searching and finding Floridan equivalents of the Swiss sites, another pioneer wetland archaeologist commenced his investigations in Britain. Although

21

other contemporary British figures acknowledged the value of wetland sites, Arthur Bulleid of Glastonbury is the founder of the archaeology of British wetlands. Bulleid set out in 1888 to identify lake settlements in the peatbogs of Somerset, and his discoveries and excavations at Glastonbury revealed the richness of a Late Iron Age occupation (Bulleid and Gray 1911, 1917). A lake village had been set amidst a marshy landscape, with a river flowing beside the palisaded settlement. There were about 90 mounds preserved on the site (interpreted as collapsed houses, sheds, workshops or other shelters) and subsequent analysis suggests that the site was occupied by 5–7 family groups each with its own prescribed area of settlement (Clarke 1972). Animal bones attest to dairying and wool production, wild birds and forest animals were often hunted, and cereals were grown on nearby dryland, with wild berries gathered seasonally. Apart from the working of stone, bronze, iron, bone and antler for tools, the inhabitants had a prolific pottery industry, made glass beads and shale bracelets, and worked extensively in wood (figure 12). Wooden buildings, fences, ladders, wagons and dugout canoes were major elements in the exploitation of the oak and ash woodlands on the dry islands and hills around the marshlands, but a wide variety of wooden bowls and tubs, dishes and spoons, handles and stoppers for vessels of clay or leather, and large notched and perforated boards (probably for looms) also demonstrate the richness of Glastonbury in archaeological terms.

The extremely wet conditions of the peatbogs which had caused the site to be abandoned encouraged Bulleid and his co-director Harold Gray in the careful excavation of structures which had been protected by the formation of peat. Stratigraphical control was perhaps better executed at the Glastonbury site than at the contemporary excavations of the Swiss, Italian and French lakeside sites or at Key Marco, but in another respect the Swiss workers were better-equipped. As we shall see, conservation of material from wetland sites is a crucial aspect, and although Bulleid and his collaborators endeavoured to conserve some artifacts, just as Cushing did, only those working in the Alpine sites made any real effort to treat waterlogged organic objects. Even so, the lowering of the water levels in the lakes of Neuchâtel and Bienne in the late nineteenth century exposed so many sites (figure 13) and yielded so much material that quantities had to be abandoned after excavations, and the Swiss record is only marginally better than that of Cushing or Bulleid.

22

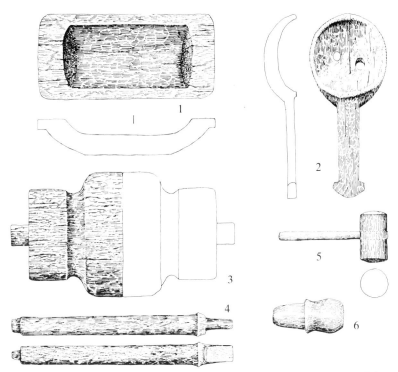

Figure 12. Artifacts of wood recovered by Arthur Bulleid from the Glastonbury lake village in the late 19th century: 1 bowl; 2 spoon or strainer; 3 axle and (4) spokes from a wagon; 5 mallet; 6 bung or stopper. (Drawn by M. Rouillard. From Coles and Orme 1980.)

Figure 13. The scene at the Mörigen lake settlement, Switzerland, in 1876, when low water levels had exposed the piles (and other artifacts) of a Late Bronze Age settlement.

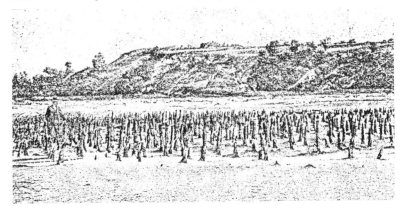

ARCHAEOLOGICAL FIELDWORK. Few textbooks of archaeology devote much attention to wetlands. Often the term 'wet site' or 'waterlogged site' is taken to infer an underwater situation with its paraphernalia of diving gear, special excavation equipment and recording methods. In some few cases this is exactly right, but in a majority it is not. The variety of wetland sites means that archaeology does not have a fixed series of techniques applicable to all of them, other than the universal one of respect for the past and recognition of the need to recover and record carefully.

Even at the fundamental level of site recognition, wetland archaeology has unique problems as well as opportunities. The examples of west coast North America show that there are many situations where waterlogging of sites can occur. Midden accumulation may block drainage systems, and thus create conditions for immersion of deposits, particularly if the old land surface is a compacted clay or silt, and therefore more or less impermeable; comparable conditions might exist in upland blanket bogs where local damming could create waterlogging. Mudslides or superficial clay slumping or deposition may bury and preserve sites, as at Ozette. Peat formation over ancient land surfaces, as in the English Fenland, and silt from rising lake levels, as in the Alpine Lakes, are two other factors leading to waterlogging. Land submergence through geological tilting, as in southern Denmark, can also lead to the total drowning of sites. There are therefore many factors involved, and the opportunities for the preservation of sites are numerous and varied. Such sites have remained protected by various degrees of waterlogging for centuries and millennia, and they will continue to be protected from developers and archaeologists so long as these anaerobic deposits remain intact. The critical period arises when this seal is broken by a variety of activities, of which the most dramatic are i) quarrying of lake muds and ii) cutting of peat; but the most destructive for archaeology is iii) the draining and desiccation of vast expanses of wetlands.

i) *Quarrying.* The recognition of archaeological evidence in wetland sites exposed by quarrying is no different from standard dryland archaeological practice. Where a new road is being built around a lake, for example, the removal of soil may reveal ancient structures which can be observed in the quarry or scraped surface, or when the road is to be constructed across the end of a lake, the off-shore deposits may be exposed in initial draining (by cofferdam) or by geological borings to test subsurface stability (Baudais, Corboud and Nierlé 1982). At Auvernier, in Lake Neuchâtel, ten different Neolithic and Bronze Age settlements have recently been discovered along the lakeshore over a distance of 2 km, through aerial photographs and mechanical boreholes prior to the activities of roadbuilding (Egloff 1977). Lakeshores are often threatened by operations such as this, but natural erosion of the shoreline can also create new exposures for archaeological observation. These quarrying operations are visibly destructive and demand a rapid archaeological response which may be met by rescue and salvage archaeology.

Dredging is underwater quarrying, and such underwater sites pose particular problems. In southern Denmark, for example, where geological tilting has submerged vast areas of former lakes and lagoons, as well as forested areas, the dredging of oyster-shell banks has often brought up prehistoric artifacts. Such sites cannot be protected, and the only solution is to maintain good contacts with the dredgers (Davidsen 1983). In south-west Funen, consistent survey by divers over the past ten years has succeeded in locating 43 settlements of the Mesolithic and Neolithic; the preservation of wooden artifacts and economic evidence on such sites is often remarkable (Skaarup 1983).

ii) *Peat cutting*. In many areas where peat is extracted for burning or fertiliser, standard terrestrial survey practices are appropriate. Instead of a gas pipeline, for example, the wetland archaeologist searches peat cuttings which may have sliced through ancient structures, once free-standing but eventually overwhelmed by peat formation. In the peat fields of Lower Saxony, for instance, which have been much reduced in the past 100 years by peat removal, an archaeological unit has been set up to search the cuttings, and record exposures of ancient trackways and other artifacts; to date nearly 300 wooden trackways, laid down to allow passage across the developing peatbog, have been discovered, dating from the fourth millennium BC up to the Middle Ages (Hayen 1980). The main difference in field survey between dryland and wetland archaeology in these circumstances is in the length of cutting to be searched and in the need for repetition of work. A simple peat field in Somerset, for example, measuring only 200 × 200 m may contain multiple 'heads' (trenches) totalling 8–10 km of peat sections to search. When cut, the peat is wet, and yields colour and texture

25

differences which alter as the peat face dries out, thus necessitating further search. The blocks of peat (called mumps, sods or turves depending on the area), stacked to dry in ruckles or ricks beside the cutting, may also contain artifacts.

These cases, lake muds and peat cuts, are quite straightforward in terms of survey, although the areas to be searched are enormous, but there are many other wetland environments where recognition problems are immense. Take, for instance, the organic-filled water-saturated muck at the Lachane site near Prince Rupert, Canada (Inglis 1976); prior to its destruction by bulldozer, the site had yielded hundreds of ancient artifacts in a rescue or salvage excavation. Following this, however, when the site was cleared by machine, not a single organic artifact was observed by archaeologists carrying out a watching brief, because the waterlogged deposits were obscured by the general messiness of the site. Yet several weeks after the commercial work had ended, rain had cleaned and exposed numbers of artifacts in the few sections left by the machine (Macdonald 1982). Adequate watching briefs and surveys in such contexts are not at all easy, and no clear solution has yet been proposed, although there is no doubt that artificial rain (hosepipes and sprinklers) is one way to expose artifacts in a wet and loose deposit.

iii) *Drainage*. By far the most destructive threat to wetlands is best described as desiccation, the drying out of waterlogged deposits. Many former marshes, swamps and peatbogs can become valuable arable or pasture if they are drained, and governments spend vast amounts of money to encourage such operations. This involves the removal of wetland vegetation by stripping, the cutting of major drainage channels, the installation of underground drains and pipes leading into such channels, and the use of pumps and barrages to encourage the flow of water from the land. The result of such actions are self-evident, in the death of wetlands. As moisture is removed, the organic peats and mucks begin to dry; their water content may have been as high as 50% volume and 95% weight, and with this removal, the deposits collapse and compact, shrink, erode and decay through biochemical oxidation. In areas where the sediments are put to the plough, the topmost peats can blow away, as in the Fenland. In areas put to grass, shrinkage takes place beneath the surface, as in Somerset, north Germany and almost every area of former wetland. Entire

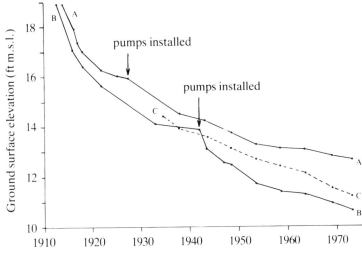

Figure 14. Results of drainage on organic soils (peats and mucks) in the Florida Everglades, USA, after initial drainage c. 1912. Note the acceleration of loss of water levels upon the installation of pumps in two of the three recorded sites. (From Stephens 1974.)

landscapes can literally and physically collapse, as in the Fenland and Florida (figure 14). When this happens and when desiccation occurs, the organic deposits, whether natural or man-made, begin to decay as the anaerobic defences are breached and then destroyed. Oxygen, bacteria, insects and other animals, fungi and other plants, invade and destroy the fabric and the character of the wetland; organic materials perish and, for archaeology, the sites assume an importance no greater, and in most cases far less, than dryland sites where there is no expectation of major organic materials. When a peatbog is first drained, the reduction in physical bulk is immense. In 1848, the landowner of Whittlesey Mere in Cambridgeshire, England, set an iron post in the peat about 1 km from the edge of the mere; this post was driven down to rest on an iron crosspiece carried on oak piles set into the underlying solid rock. The top of the post was exactly level with the surface of the peat in 1848, and as drainage of the mere progressed, the shrinkage of the peat body could be observed (figure 15). By 1860, the surface of the peat had fallen by 1.45 m, by 1870 it had shrunk a further 0.9 m, and by 1892 the total fall was over 3 m (Godwin 1978).

27

At the Belle Glade Center in Florida, a concrete post was set into bedrock in 1924, with its top flush with the ground surface; by 1974 a loss by shrinkage of 1.37 m had been recorded, with again the most dramatic loss occurring within the first decades of drainage (Stephens 1974). It must be emphasised that these recorded falls are due entirely to shrinkage of the peat through drainage some distance away from the recording sites, and not to the physical removal of the organic deposits.

There is one other phenomenon attached to such. drainage operations. If the area thus drained is put into cultivation, and not left as permanent grassland, then wind erosion of the loose dry particles of organic peat, which are extremely light, can be serious, and bog-blows will almost totally obscure the light on occasions, as centimetres of deposit are physically removed and deposited downwind many kilometres away. Fieldwork across peatbogs may therefore detect nothing in a flat landscape, but as shrinkage and erosion occurs, ancient structures sealed by peat may begin to protrude above the surface; any site set upon an old land surface and subsequently covered by peat will shrink less than the peat and will begin to protrude from a landscape which was completely flat at first sight. In the Fenland of eastern England, consistent fieldwork over several years can now document the appearance of drowned burial mounds of the Bronze Age (Hall 1981), and what was apparently a barren landscape 10 years ago is now known to contain entire prehistoric barrow cemeteries. Where the fieldwork is combined with surveys of drainage

Figure 15. The Holme Fen post, Cambridgeshire, England. The top of the post was flush with the surface of the peat in 1848, and shrinkage of the peat through nearby drainage has been over 3 m.

28

ditches and bore-holes where vertical stratigraphies can be recorded, a beginning can be made towards the identification of successive landscapes, some occupied by man, others marking periods where human activities were limited by true wetland conditions (figures 16, 17). Other wetlands are not so easily worked by field survey. Many are now sealed by metres of recent silts, or clays. These are unlikely to shrink in a uniform and dramatic way, and their weight may well have crushed or at least compressed the underlying waterlogged deposits. If the clay or silt dries severely and cracks, then contamination will be introduced into the deposits beneath. Drainage or river channels through the area may allow some archaeological inspection, but fieldwork in these areas is extremely difficult and unlikely to be fully representative. Parts of the Somerset Levels are sealed in this way, and areas of lakeside settlement in the Alpine region as well.

The realisation that such events are occurring, and that archaeological sites (as well as wetland plants and animals) are threatened, may encourage field survey and the listing and scheduling of particular sites which seem to be important to save for the future. This is laudable but the point is not always taken that to legally protect a wetland site and not to encourage and ensure the maintenance of the wetland itself is a pointless exercise. Waterlogged sites will decay beneath the surface of the former wetland, if desiccation is allowed in and around the site. The effect of legislation is therefore sometimes to prevent archaeological and even conservation efforts, and to permit a site to inexorably decay completely unseen beneath the ground. 'The law is an ass' is certainly true in these cases. To protect a wetland site for the future involves far more than a piece of archaeological legislation, and it must include contributions from other conservancy councils and planning authorities to ensure the preservation of the whole wetland environment.

Figures 16, 17 (overleaf). Maps of Manea parish, Cambridgeshire, England. Figure 16 shows the state of knowledge before fieldwork began, with three sites: A Roman pottery; B Roman pewter; 7 cropmarks from aerial photographs. Figure 17 represents the information gained by intensive field survey: C macehead (Mesolithic); D flint scatter; E flint barbed arrowhead of type normally found with burials; 1, 2, 8 flint scatters (Mesolithic); 3, 9 flint scatters (Early Bronze Age); 4 flint scatter; 5, 6 Iron Age and Roman sites; 10 barrow excavated c. 1929 but never reported; 7 cropmark of ring ditch site. The water courses shown are the extent of Neolithic fen, preserved by silting. (Maps produced by D. N. Hall.)

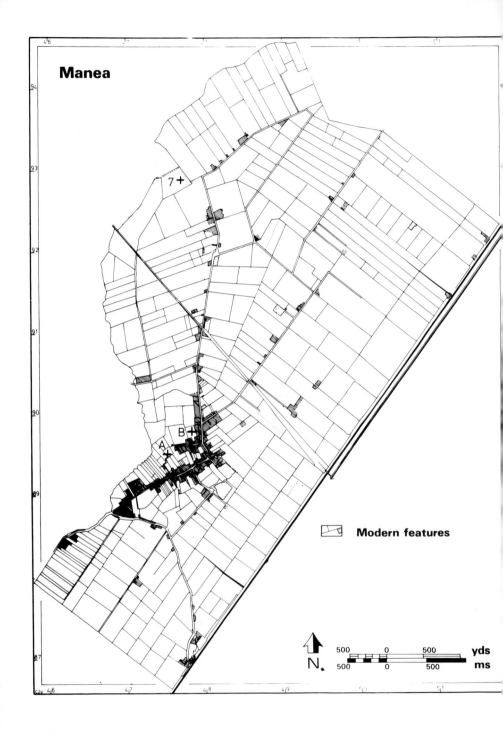

Manea

7+

B+

A+

Modern features

N.

| 500 | 0 | 500 | yds |
| 500 | 0 | 500 | ms |

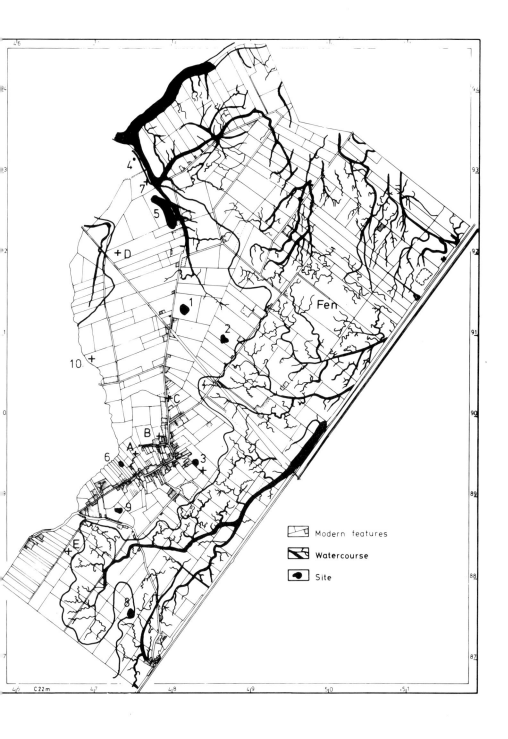

Fen

Modern features

Watercourse

Site

C 22 m

Techniques. Although many detection devices have been developed for archaeology, such as resistivity, magnetic and aerial surveys, few appear to work reliably in waterlogged deposits where the essential element of water effectively drowns the variations. Wet peat, wet mud and wet wood are not often sufficiently different for such methods to succeed (but see Lenihan 1981). Coring is often a useful mechanism for determining general stratigraphies in wetlands, and also for more detailed tracing of linear structures (Coles and Orme 1980).

Aerial photography in a desiccated wetland can yield useful information, as ancient monuments, constructed of sand, earth or stones, emerge from the uniformly dark peats, and are detected by colour changes. As important is the identification of extinct river courses and peat/clay interfaces which help to recreate the patterns of environmental change in these wetlands (figure 17). More spectacular are the aerial photographs of Swiss Bronze Age settlements, marked by piles and posts, and visible beneath 2–4 m of the cold clear water of Lake Neuchâtel in winter (Egloff 1981; Arnold 1982) (figures 18, 19).

One technique for field survey which appears promising is subsurface sonar or radar; the detection of heavy wooden structures, as well as drowned forests of stumps and fallen trees (bog oaks), seems to be well within the limits of precision of the method, but its main use is likely to be in mapping the contours of bedrock or other hard deposits beneath the softer peats and silts of wetlands (Jørgensen 1982; Geophysical Survey Systems n.d.).

Any field survey is only as good as 'ground control', the field officers on the ground, and for wetland archaeology there can be no dispute over this. Four main areas of work can be identified, each linked with the others:

1) Because of the variable nature of wetlands deposits, reliance cannot be placed on non-archaeologists working the land, who may either not see, or not report, discoveries made by accident. An archaeological presence is imperative. A good example of this is in the extraordinary discoveries of Neolithic field systems in Co. Mayo, Ireland (figure 55), uncovered entirely by local peat-cutters over many years but only recognised as important by an observant amateur archaeologist (Caulfield 1983).

2) The character of wetland sites is often difficult to define and many presumptive reports of discoveries turn out to be nothing

32

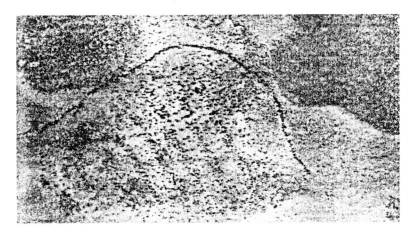

Figures 18, 19. Aerial photograph and plan of the Late Bronze Age settlement at Cortaillod, Switzerland, with the piles forming clearly-defined alignments (structures and streets) beneath the still waters of the Lake of Neuchatel. (From Arnold 1982.)

33

more than naturally occurring deposits such as drowned woodland, clay flood lenses and the like. Only by persistent fieldwork will discoveries and reports be systematically sifted and results achieved with some confidence. Wetland work in pubs, for example, is often rewarded by local information, a good combination of thirsts for both knowledge and liquids. The first information about the Neolithic hurdles from Walton Heath, Somerset, was obtained in a pub only hours after their discovery by a peat-cutter (Coles and Orme 1980). And the author was informed about a series of ancient bog-roads in Co. Offaly, Ireland, within five minutes of entering a local hostelry. The point is equally true that wetland sites are often slight and can be transitory; the need to be on the spot for information and verification is obvious.

3) The understanding of wetland deposits is not easily gained. Peat as a term covers a multitude of organic sediments, as do flooding silts and clays and muds. For adequate field survey in wetlands, an intimate knowledge of the local deposits is imperative, and this can only be acquired by experience of the local topography and environmental history. No archaeological site is as dependent upon environmental information as a wetland one.

4) Yet because wetlands cover vast expanses of the world, and are being attacked by quarrying, cutting and drainage (figure 20) archaeologists can never cope with all the areas requiring surveillance, and they must rely therefore upon local informants (notwithstanding the remarks in 1) above), old records of earlier discoveries, and their own knowledge of the landscapes acquired through fieldwork and environmental analyses. In this way, identification of known localities, and predictions of likely sites, can encourage concentrated efforts on particular areas. This approach has been notably successful in the Somerset Levels, and north German moors, the Fenlands, and the Florida wetlands, in all areas where invisible sites have been 'identified' prior to their actual exposure through shrinkage or removal of peat and muck; archaeological recovery techniques can thus be geared in readiness. In Florida, the identification of lenses of higher and drier ground in a wetland 'sea' of swamps and lakes, through infra-red aerial photographs, has led to predictions about human occupations at many specific positions on the island edges, and these have been confirmed

by fieldwork prior to their disintegration through drainage and other developments of the region (Purdy 1982). In Somerset, the location of flint scatters on islands and hill slopes, and the interpretation of pollen analyses, have led to accurate predictions of platforms and trackways which served such dryland occupation sites.

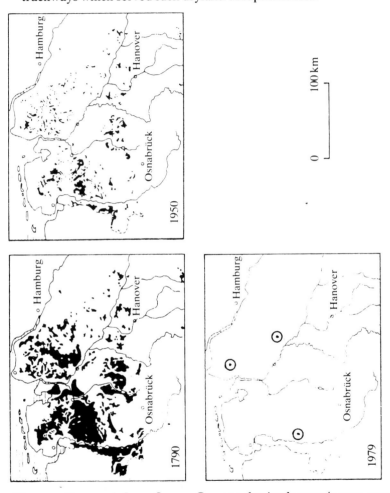

Figure 20. Peat moss in Lower Saxony, Germany, showing the extent in 1790, 1950 and 1979. The three spots in 1979 are the only areas where upper peats and original surfaces survive. (From Hayen 1980.)

2

Methods

SENSITIVITY ANALYSIS. Many wetland sites have been excavated in the past, and it is a truism to say that each is unique. Every site will have special characteristics, particular degrees of wetness and acidity, so that no standard manual of excavation procedures can be prescribed. The mental approach to a flat dryland site has to be discarded, and a three-dimensional expectation introduced. Instead of postholes, expect to find posts (figure 9); instead of leached or damaged occupation surfaces, expect to find living floors (figure 21); instead of wall trenches, expect to find parts of walls either fallen over or still standing (figure 8); instead of stone tools, expect to find wooden implements and stone blades in their hafts (figure 60); instead of stains and dark patches, expect to find fragments of textiles, hides, wooden plates (figure 12); instead of palisade trenches, expect to find wattles (figure 22), or the bases of poles; instead of beaten paths, expect to find wooden roads or bridge bases (figure 2); instead of bones and stains, expect to find wooden coffins, biers, perhaps hair and skin as well as bone, or wooden effigies (figure 11).

There are, however, certain fundamental principles, and it is appropriate to consider these under the broad heading of *sensitivity analysis,* which is basically a disciplined and experimental approach to wetland archaeology. Each site is assessed on the basis of its known features, on the following lines:

1) Preliminary site *identification* (e.g. settlement, burial, platform) and *chronological position.* This may determine its priority for extensive examination, dependent upon current knowledge.

2) Site *content,* the types of evidence likely to be present (e.g. palisade, house foundations, burial pits or platform, materials, artifacts). This again will influence the course of action to be taken.

3) *Condition* of the site, i.e. the degree of wetness and the nature of the containing deposit. This will certainly be of fundamental importance in the decisions about work to be undertaken. A heavily-

36

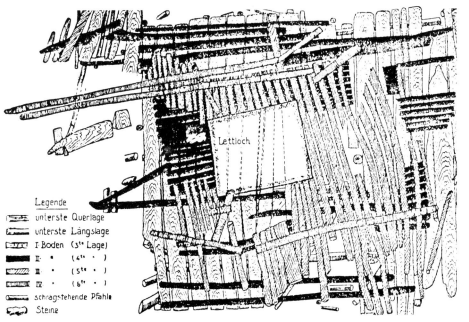

Legende
≥ unterste Querlage
unterste Längslage
I·Boden (3ᵗᵉ Lage)
II· " (4ᵗᵉ ")
III· " (5ᵗᵉ ")
IV· " (6ᵗᵉ ")
schrägstehende Pfähle
Steine

Figure 21. Complexity and preservation of house flooring at a Neolithic settlement in Wauwilermoos, Switzerland, recorded in 1903-06 excavations. (From Speck 1981.)

waterlogged site in soft peats will be a better proposition than a partly-desiccated site in a hardened silt or mud, but only if the priority accorded on the basis of site identification and content is high.

4) *Recovery* techniques to be used. This requires very careful assessment, and among the relevant factors are the experience and skill of the team, its rate of excavation (speed of operations), the sampling strategies, on-site conservation, and general preparation and expectation. These matters are discussed below.

5) Requirements for *post-excavation* work. This is probably the most crucial element in any programme, and unless it is fully debated and agreed beforehand, and arrangements made, the excavation should not proceed. Sampling and extraction of materials for analyses, specialists and their specific requirements, and relevance of such work to the project's aims, must be laid down and fully understood by all.

Figure 22. The Eclipse Track, Somerset, England, during excavation in 1981. The track was discovered during fieldwork, and was made of overlapping hurdles c. 1800 BC.

6) *Conservation* needs, both for artifactual materials and site location. Wetland sites are fragile, and vulnerable to decay and inadvertent destruction, and the interest of the public as well as of the archaeologists and conservators must be taken into account. To spend vast sums on the acquisition of a wetland site, only to find plans well advanced for the drainage of immediately adjacent lands, is probably pointless in the long run. To recover large amounts of fragile artifacts requiring immediate treatment and then to find no resource available or willing to undertake the work is to waste time and effort.

All of these aspects of the pre-excavation analysis are important, and it is futile to undertake a large-scale wetland operation without extensive preparations.

38

Figure 23. Excavations on the Sweet Track, Somerset. The excavators work from planks held over the wet site. Plastic sheets protect the wood from drying, and particular elements are bagged individually.

ACCESS AND WATER. The principles determined, the actual process of recovery may commence, and here there can be many problems, some perhaps anticipated but others which will emerge unexpectedly. Wetland sites are by their nature not often suitable even for normal archaeological movement on site, i.e. on the ground itself, or on baulks, or on planks laid on the site. Movement has to be restricted and often kept to plankwalks held clear of the actual deposits being worked, through elaborate and seemingly precarious systems of boxes and planks strategically placed. Excavation work itself is generally carried out from planks suspended over the site, or from toe-boards placed on the deposits where small clear areas exist (figure 23). Sometimes the major problem is of access to the deposits, if a site consists of vast expanses of collapsed wooden pieces in sodden state, each in crucial association with its neighbours. Ingenuity in such circumstances is a fundamental requirement, and caution too.

39

There is also a clear need for rigorous and vigorous supervision. On occasion, as probably on every archaeological excavation, slips will occur, and excavators may tumble from a suspended plank, or step carelessly off a toe-board, onto and into the organic deposits. Damage will be done, of course, but in almost every case more damage will be caused by the uncontrolled rapid attempt to get out than by the actual fall. Struggling to get out can be fatal to fragile structures, and could also be so for the poor worker if he or she is not disciplined enough to remain still, in a fallen state, until extraction can be achieved with care under the direction of a fellow worker. Undisciplined archaeologists, or unthinking workers, are lethal on a wet site; one rule advanced in peatbog excavations in Somerset, for example, was never to stand on the wet peat surface being worked ('no feet on peat' was the expression), until one worker obeyed it by standing on the prehistoric wood being uncovered. His fate remains secret, but wet-site archaeologists are always anxious to find out what happens to human bodies buried in the wet.

The procedures developed for the excavation of water-saturated sites on the west coast of North America are of interest and value. The investigation of the settlement buried by mudslides at Ozette was among the first to employ hydraulic techniques (Gleeson and Grosso 1976), and these were further refined by work at Axeti (Hobler 1976), Lachane (Inglis 1976) and Little Qualicum, all British Columbia (Bernick 1983). At Ozette, a site beside the Pacific Ocean, pumps were used to provide sea water (at c.40 gallons per minute at 250 lbs pressure) to wash off the heavy clay overburden as well as to loosen and clean the materials in the cultural deposits. During winter work, heavy surf prevented such sea-based pumps from working, and a very successful system was devised for gravity-feed from freshwater streams above the site; water was fed into ponds and thence into holding tanks from which a constant pressure could be obtained (through a pump) to hoses. The hose nozzles were adjustable for the types of deposits being worked, with a feedback into the tanks at low pressures.

At Axeti, a series of intertidal deposits where some horizontal displacement of artifacts was suspected, large areas of the site were hosed, then inspected for features and finds, before cleaning with smaller water sprays; and loss of position by high pressure water was judged less important than the investigation of a large area of the site.

40

The Lachane site, a midden and refuse dump, was also worked with water (figure 24) and basketry was cleaned with fine trigger sprays, dental tools (including sharpened wooden tongue depressors – like lolly or popsicle sticks) and recorded and analysed *in situ* (cf. figure 25), before being sewn into nylon mesh and sealed in plastic for shipment and conservation. All of these sites demonstrate the success of water as an excavation agent in mud, sand and shell deposits.

Such pumps, pipes, tanks and sprays are expensive to install and keep in operation, but their value is far in excess of their cost, if measured in terms of the recognition of features and stratigraphical units, the identification and recovery of small artifacts, the exposure and retrieval of animal remains, and the recognition and analysis *in situ* of badly-decayed organic objects such as textiles and basketry.

One final point should be made about the use of large quantities of water in excavating or sieving deposits. Recycling of water is possible, but eventually many tonnes of water may be released on the environment; if heavily impregnated with particles of organic or inorganic origin, pollution is a danger.

Figure 24. Excavation with water sprays at the Lachane site, British Columbia. The midden deposits were loose enough to be cleared away by variable water pressures, and finely-worked wooden and other artifacts were exposed by this method. (Photo G. Macdonald.)

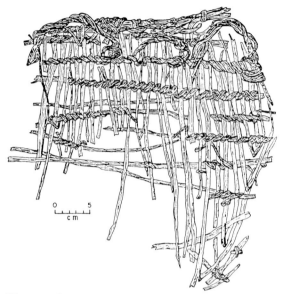

Figure 25. Open wrapped twining basketry from the Little Qualicum River site, British Columbia, Canada. Exposed and excavated by water spray, and recorded in situ *before lifting for conservation. The fragile nature of such fibres, mostly red cedar bark, requires extreme delicacy in excavation to avoid losing important details of weave and ties. (From Bernick 1983.)*

Here it might also be noted that any excavation of a wet or water-logged site will introduce drainage into the site and the area around it. If a trench, for example, is cut through or into a wet deposit, and then left either open or backfilled loosely, drainage from the adjacent wet deposits will commence immediately, and in time the water table will be lowered. Thus to excavate into a waterlogged archaeological site is to initiate its destruction, and once the decision has been taken to examine a site, a full programme must be planned rather than merely a test or *sondage* into the heart of the evidence. Backfilling of wetland deposits is no real solution to this, and in fact backfilling for ordinary reasons is also a major problem, as the intrusive material is most unlikely to consolidate and bind with the original undisturbed sections, and may remain a threat to heavy animals and machinery for years. This is no advertisement for archaeological goodwill to farmers and other landusers.

42

UNDERWATER SITES. Some of the most spectacular wetland sites excavated in recent years have been beneath the waters of lakes or sea; the Mesolithic settlement at Tybrind Vig in Denmark, the Neolithic and Bronze Age settlements at Lake Paladru, France, and the Lakes of Neuchâtel and Zürich, provide excellent examples of underwater techniques. The site of Tybrind Vig (vig = cove or small bay) was first found by amateur divers and lies 250 m from the present coast at 2.5–3.0 m below sea level (Andersen 1980). The excavations were conducted exactly as they would have been on land with minimal differences. A fixed grid of one-metre squares was laid out on the sea bed, all finds were plotted in three dimensions with average sea level used as a benchmark horizon, and standard sampling procedures were used for environmental analyses. Vertical sections of the 1 m of organic deposits could be cut and maintained. One positive advantage of working such a site under water is that the excavators can operate from positions above the site, and no elaborate supports, planking or toe-boards are required. In the lifting of heavy or fragile objects, the water medium is also a distinct advantage, and movement up to the support pontoon (figure 26) is relatively easy for such artifacts. Visibility at this site has been generally good, with calm and cold waters.

Figure 26. The pontoon at Tybrind Vig, Denmark, positioned over the site which lies c. 3 m below the surface. The steel platform (5 × 4 m) holds a compressor for the pumps used to clear the digging area on the sea floor. (Photo S. Andersen.)

43

At Auvernier in Switzerland, where motorway building threatened a number of sites, teams of divers initiated excavations on two Late Bronze Age settlements until dams could be built to allow the sites to be drained and excavated in the open air (Strahm 1976; Arnold 1977). Other sites were enclosed by banks or coffer dams which subsequently made up part of the infilling for the motorway foundations.

One piece of indispensable equipment for such sites is a pump capable of expelling large amounts of water. The Swiss experience here and in Lake Zürich (Ruoff 1981d), on working both underwater and above water, allows comparisons of cost as well as results, and a preliminary comment is that the construction of a coffer dam in relatively shallow water provides a cheaper method of excavation overall, than the organisation of a full-scale underwater excavation will entail. One of the sites at Auvernier was enclosed by a series of interlocking metal plates forming an area of 10×20 m for excavation; water pressure on the walls was found to be extremely high even in shallow conditions, so there is a safety factor involved here which cannot be ignored. Inside such enclosures, small ditches or sumps collected water for pumping away, and the excavations themselves have been described as of humid terrestrial character.

The Neolithic settlement of Charavines in Lake Paladru, France, was first exposed during an exceptionally dry period in 1921 but it was not until 1971 that systematic work could begin (Bocquet 1982; Bocquet et al. 1976). The results have been extraordinary even by wetland standards, but it is the techniques of work that are relevant here. Teams of amateur divers first mapped the upstanding wooden piles of the settlement (figure 27), and tagged them in such a way that aerial photographs could outline the extent of the site, supported by trial excavations. As the settlement lies under 2–4 m of water in normal conditions, the major excavations have created many problems, among them the knowledge that the divers working on the site progressively deteriorate during their periods under water, so that disorientation and loss of accuracy in, e.g. recording can be serious (see Baddeley 1971). Careful scheduling and checking of results are necessary, in a way that might perhaps be appropriate on dryland excavations in sustained hot conditions. At Charavines, most of the excavation of the thick deposits of silt and organic muds takes place in summer months when the waters of the lake are warmer, and when

44

Figure 27. Neolithic wooden piles from the Charavines settlement beneath the waters of Lake Paladru, France, with the excavation grid tapes in place. (Photo F. Vin.)

plankton and calcium carbonates are in suspension, thus reducing visibility. The excavation of the deposits also releases silt particles. In order to reduce the difficulties thus created, a curtain of water is created around the excavation unit which carries away much of the suspended matter. The curtain is created by water forced at pressure through pipes with multiple minute holes, which form currents flowing away from the excavation units being worked.

The site is divided into units of 5 m, but instead of squares, triangles are used. A metal triangular frame with 5 m sides is fixed to the overall site grid, with each apex holding a measuring tape. Finds and features as uncovered are measured in from all three points. Each of these large triangles is further subdivided by strings at 1 m intervals, forming 25 sub-units which are used for sampling and general recording. The recording of features and finds *in situ* is by crayon upon rigid sheets of PVC pre-labelled with the sub-unit sides and designation, which fit over the frame, and notes are written directly upon these sheets. Almost all of the actual excavation is carried out by hand, without metal tools, although the lifting of finds and samples in blocks involves metal plates beneath. Samples for stratigraphical control are taken by the insertion of tubes (10–20 cm diameter) through the sediments, just as cores would be taken by borer on terrestrial sites. The sediments and artifacts removed in the excavation process are taken by bucket or box to the pontoon above the site which acts as site office, recording centre, rest area, and pivot for the entire operation.

These few examples demonstrate that there is no such thing as a wetland excavation which can be used as a pattern for work on other wetland sites. Every site has its own problems and opportunities. However, there is one basic threat which is applicable to every wetland site whether it be under or above water, and that is the threat of drying-out of those parts of the site which are exposed to the air. For underwater sites, the danger comes when materials are floated to the surface of the water; for terrestrial sites, the threat is ever-present, as soon as the materials are exposed on the site.

RECOVERY, RECORDING AND CONSERVATION. There is one fundamental rule for wet sites: keep it wet. It is obvious that any wetland site may be full of wet wood, bark and leaves, soggy pottery, soft bone, fragile elements such as fishscales, beetle wing-cases, seeds, textiles and pieces of hide; in these circumstances, to allow the evidence to dry out is negligent, to say the least, and some measure must be adopted to keep the evidence in its original as-found state, and to avoid the alteration of damp-dry-damp-dry conditions which will destroy much.

The extraction of waterlogged materials, or even objects of metal or clay, from an underwater site involves a heavy investment in conservation, although what is called on-site conservation is clearly not much of a problem. For a terrestrial wet site, however, the problems may be very great and can be countered by continuous or regular spraying of the site, flooding it deliberately, or protecting it entirely or partly by sealing with plastic sheeting (figure 28). Black sheeting is not recom-

46

Figure 28. Excavations in a Neolithic causewayed enclosure at Etton, Cambridgeshire, England. The ditches are waterlogged and contain abundant wood and other organic refuse. The deposits are maintained in a damp state by liberal use of polythene sheeting, and damp sponge and foam rubber panels. Note the metal frames for erecting or dismantling canvas or plastic covers over parts of the site. (Photo F. Pryor.)

mended as this absorbs heat and may create a humid but too-warm environment beneath. In emergencies, damp foam sheets, heaps of moss, or layers of wet newspapers can help to conserve moisture in a waterlogged structure, but there are problems in the removal of such materials from delicate artifacts or deposits for analysis. The age of wetland archaeology is surely also the age of the polythene sheet. No one has yet taken the logical step on a terrestrial wetland site, by building a coffer dam around it, completely flooding it, and then excavating it under water. Problems of keeping the site damp, of lifting artifacts, and of keeping the excavators off the site, would all be solved.

The excavation tools for wetland sites will vary, depending upon the matrix of mud, silt, clay, muck or peat, and the range and condition of the materials to be recovered. Dried or drying deposits may be extremely intractable, requiring the spade and trowel, with consequent likelihood of damage to artifacts buried within them. Softer deposits of wet muds or peats will permit, indeed necessitate, the use of more delicate tools such as flat wooden scrapers, spatulae, and bare fingers. Hand-digging of wet deposits means just that, as sensitivity to changes in the compacting of the deposits may signal a buried artifact, either small or structural. Sight, sound and feel are all indicative of the nature of deposits. In a very wet deposit, such as peat, a moment's delay will sometimes allow very slight shrinkage of deposits, permitting precise separation and identification of different materials; a slight crack may appear between a piece of wet wood and its surrounding peat, even if both are in a very soggy state.

The use of water sprays may allow sediments to be washed gently from features and finds, and in very dense middens this has been found to be successful (figure 24), as also for the cleaning of large pieces of timber. The uncontrolled use of a spray, too forceful or misdirected, is dangerous. The sediments removed by careful spraying can be collected by vacuum or sump and sieved for organic particles (figure 29), and a good measure of experience in water manipulation is important. Contamination of wet deposits is a real hazard, particularly if a section through a wet site is being worked, as material will be washed down the faces from upper levels, or brought in from elsewhere by wind, water or feet, and any samples of the deposits for radiocarbon analysis may well be contaminated.

Figure 29. Fine sieving of midden samples from Hontoon Island, Florida. Baskets of material are removed from the site and carefully sprayed through variable mesh sizes to recover small artifacts, vertebrate remains, leaves and twigs. (Photo B. Purdy.)

If there is one rule for digging wetland sites it is that there can be no mechanical excavation, by which is meant unattentive scraping of deposits by either machines or humans. The use of real mechanical equipment, long-arm diggers for example, is possible for the removal of substantial overburdens, but the weight of the bucket on such arms can cause serious compression even as it gently digs or scoops, and of course the machine itself near a wet site may spell future trouble. In all wet sites taken to a depth exceeding 1 m, careful shoring of the excavation walls is essential. Bulging walls full of moisture are dangerous, and bursters and mud flows are potentially dangerous.

Recording. The recording of structures, features and other artifacts during excavation should be standard, with full three-dimensional references taken. Wetland sites tend to have a real third dimension, in

49

that many vertical pieces are represented not only by their postholes but also by the upper parts of the post. The inter-relationships of multiple series of such vertical pieces which may penetrate many horizons of occupation can pose enormous problems, and both careful stratigraphic control and tree-ring analysis are essential (figures 30, 31).

In practice, the use of pinned metal or plastic labels on all components of a structure, or series of horizons, allows notes and records to be made of associations and positions prior to the dismantling of a complex; for wooden structures such as a waterfront, platform, trackway, wattle-work panel, or even a simple bundle of wood, three-dimensional recording has to be devised and made to work. Mechanical three-dimensional recording will not work without context. Multiple photographs and 'instant' photographs for annotation are useful, but stereoscopic pairs are likely to be invaluable. Immediate off-site photography is in some ways more difficult, due to the need to keep the waterlogged artifacts wet and yet to achieve adequate lighting to illustrate the salient points of interest.

A more fundamental problem in recording concerns the location of the site itself. In the course of fieldwork in a peatbog, for example, part of a structure may be noted and recorded in relation to nearby points and levelled into an adjacent Bench Mark or fixed point of altitude, generally in relation to mean sea level. In subsequent years, other parts of the structure may also be noted through continued peat-cutting and fieldwork, but it may prove difficult to relate the original now-gone findspot to the later finds, because the bog has not only shrunk but has shifted sideways; the levelling mark may also have sunk, particularly if a temporary mark has been chosen on any structure placed upon the peat. The differences may be slight, but might be

Figure 30. Outline of the elements making up the organic and inorganic deposits at the Bronze Age settlement of Auvernier, Switzerland: 1 stones; 2 clay; 3 plant remains; 4 fine gravel and sand. This sedimentation is observable on lake shores in the region today; upon these sediments at Auvernier, the lakeside settlement was constructed, with heavy piles driven through the deposits. (From Strahm 1976.)

Figure 31. Schematic representation of the complications of stratigraphy at the Steinberge settlement, Bierlersee, Switzerland: A) the remains of the settlement overwhelmed by water and sand and silt deposit; B) with fallen lake levels the deposits are eroded, and imperishables are lowered to the top of the surviving deposits; C) the site is again flooded, with smoothing of the top deposits, and archaeologists awaited. (From Speck 1981.)

50

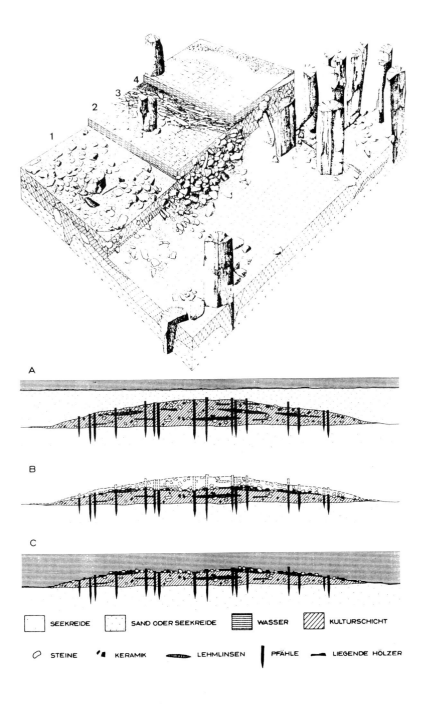

SEEKREIDE   SAND ODER SEEKREIDE   WASSER   KULTURSCHICHT

STEINE   KERAMIK   LEHMLINSEN   PFÄHLE   LIEGENDE HÖLZER

important. The same effects may also be encountered in lake muds, where shrinkage, compaction, or sheering may cause substantial movement of the deposits in which the structure lay. In other words, some wetlands have no fixed usable reference points in any dimension, as a glance at any large raised bog in central Ireland, or blanket bog in highland Britain, will soon make clear. Here is where a lengthy experience and closely-detailed knowledge of the landscape can be invaluable, and generally a combination of good surveying practice and understanding of the environment can overcome such difficulties. The firm answer is to sink sturdy posts through the wet deposits into the bedrock, but often this is not possible from the point of view of expense, and sometimes the initial sighting of a structure may be so slight that the trouble seems excessive. The development of an overall plan of Neolithic field systems, settlements and tombs in Co. Mayo, Ireland, has to rely upon reference points established over wide areas so that new exposures can be incorporated in the archaeological plans, and here a combination of known reference points and good sound surveying can surmount the problems.

In the course of excavation, artifacts in a wide variety of materials and conditions will be exposed, and their conservation will immediately pose problems. The diagram shows two simplified sequences of events which occur when an artifact comes to be buried or abandoned (figure 32). At first, decay in a dryland is dramatic (i) as the artifact attempts to stablise with the new environment which has been created for it. On a wet site, the decay is prevented (ii) for most substances. In time each artifact reaches a position of stability where decay is halted (iii). At the moment of discovery, by archaeologist or others, a new situation is created, and decay will begin again, perhaps only slightly for an artifact in a dryland site (iv), but very dramatically and critically if the object is wrenched from its wetland cushion (v). Here is where the fragility of wetland sites becomes evident, and unless the archaeologist has the fundamental experience and equipment to halt this decay, his endeavours will have succeeded only in the destruction of the evidence that he set out to recover (figure 33). There are several guides to on-site conservation (e.g. Dowman 1970), but the rule is simple: if wet, keep wet; if damp, keep damp; if dry, keep dry.

The yield of wetland sites can be immense. A small area excavation (3 × 3 m) in a Florida settlement site yielded 5777 bones from 48

52

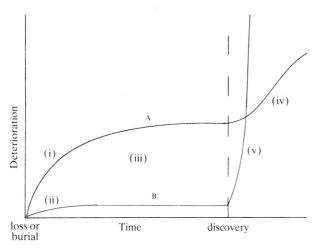

loss or burial | Time | discovery

Figure 32. Deterioration of organic artifacts following loss or burial over time and through discovery: A) material on a dry site will deteriorate rapidly (and may disappear) but may eventually reach a position of stability which is broken by discovery and will lead to further decay; B) material on a waterlogged site will barely decay until discovery or exposure to air, when very rapid deterioration will begin. On-site conservation is essential to arrest such decay.

Figure 33. A wooden mask from the Key Marco site, Florida, USA. This mask was discovered over 80 years ago and originally was comparable in form to that shown in figure 11; the lack of conservation on this specimen has resulted in cracking and distortion. (Photo B. Purdy.)

53

animal species, 3624 pieces of wood of 25 plant species, and 3265 potsherds, from a deposit only 1.5 m thick (Purdy 1982) (figure 34). To separate, sieve and hand-sort the vertebrate and invertebrate animals, the seeds and leaves, the woods and the inorganic finds, and to extract and identify the pollen from a small sample of any wetland site is a combined task far exceeding in its requirements the time actually taken to excavate the site. A wet site may be easy to dig, but its study is always lengthy and complex. Standard practices on dryland sites for the retrieval of small artifacts (stone tools, pottery) and bone are appropriate for wetland sites if the material is firm enough for physical removal. But wetland sites will also contain, in fact often consist of, substantial wooden structures or parts thereof. To record and then discard such evidence because it is not 'small finds' is not good enough, granted the diminishing number of well-preserved wetland sites that exist. Every effort must be made to save significant parts of such sites for future study or display. Wetland structures are just those parts of archaeology which are instantly identifiable to the public, as they need no hypothetical reconstruction. A wattle-panel, house floor, or boat, is there to see, maybe even to touch, and one archaeologist has said: 'It may be the wet and frozen site archaeologists who save the neck, in terms of public support, of those archaeologists . . . whose results are totally incomprehensible to the public' (Macdonald 1982). There is a fine double meaning here, as most wetland field archaeologists will acknowledge.

The actual lifting of heavy waterlogged parts of a site should pose no problems, with the use of modern planks or metal sheets beneath a fragile object, and liberal padding and bandaging. For collapsed structural pieces such as wattle-work or walling, such lifting may not be possible and moulds of various rubber compounds may have to be taken instead (Spriggs 1982). All of this takes time but is well worth the expense in the long term. An obvious danger in block lifting is the loss of information about the underlying deposit which may be truncated horizontally in the operation. Only the archaeologist on site can determine if the potential loss of contextual information is worth the effort of retrieving a cumbersome object in one piece or in articulation. It is a galling situation when such an effort has been made, and then the artifact has to be neatly sectioned to fit into holding or conservation tanks; such events are happily no longer with us (?), but the archaeo-

54

Figure 34. Excavations at Hontoon Island, Florida, USA. Samples from a midden are being water sieved for recovery of major elements such as bone, wood and pottery. Note the swampy environment. (Photo courtesy of B. Purdy.)

logist will have to determine his course of action soon after the discovery. One of the Mesolithic logboats at Tybrind Vig, Denmark, was in a damaged state and had to be sawn into manageable portions for lifting to the surface of the water and conservation (figure 35); this seems an entirely logical course of action in the circumstances, but on a terrestrial site the necessity of such an operation may need greater explanation.

CONSERVATION. On-site and off-site conservation is a fundamental part of any wetland excavation, and any large-scale wetland excavation team that does not have close contact or collaboration with conservators, and laboratory facilities within a day's journey, should not be allowed to operate.

This book is in no way a manual of conservation, and permanent consolidation of materials is a matter for trained conservators. The archaeologist must, however, maintain the artifacts as found and record their on-site treatment for the conservator to reverse or accentuate as he or she see fit. There is every reason to suggest that conservators should be on-site from the beginning of excavation, to advise and take charge of the specialist work of protection, lifting and transport of artifacts to the laboratory. Conservation is rarely a task which should be assumed by the archaeologist unless as a last resort. When we consider that a Neolithic wooden trackway in a peatbog (the Sweet Track) may contain over 10000 pieces of worked wood, or part of a Bronze Age lakeside settlement (Auvernier) may yield a tonne of wet pottery, 150 woven baskets, 400 bronze objects, we can begin to gauge the problems. The medieval town of Novgorod in Russia, excavated for many decades, has yielded tens of thousands of wooden artifacts (Thompson 1967). Should all of these be saved by expensive conservation processes? The debate is hardly begun, and much has been and is being lost; further comment appears in the Conclusion.

There is one fundamental point, however. Artifacts which are exposed during excavation must be recorded (by photography, drawing and notes) before they are immersed in any conservation process. Subtle or substantial alterations may occur during conservation, and there is never a better time to record an artifact than upon its discovery; cleaning off-site will often, of course, expose new features, but other aspects may be reduced in clarity. It is not sufficient to assume that all details can be distinguished after the object has been exposed and removed and conserved; this is particularly true for wood. A strict regime is required for the continuous assessment of artifacts as they move from on-site to off-site facilities, including storage.

Among the various conservation processes developed over the past fifty years for waterlogged materials (particularly wet wood) impregnation by polyethylene glycol (PEG) in different grades of molecular weight is still one of the most reliable. The process involves replace-

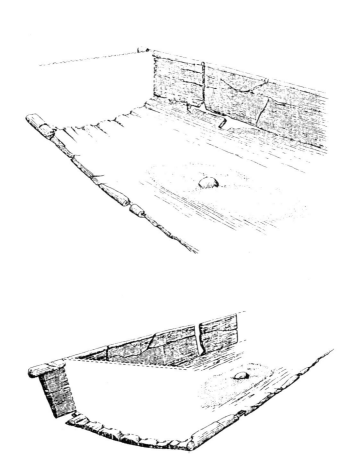

Figure 35. Reconstruction drawing and detail of the stern of one of the Mesolithic dugouts from Tybrind Vig, Denmark. The boat was made from a straight-grown lime with very few knots. The clay and sand patch shown is where fires were lit, probably for eel fishing. The boat was lifted from the seabed in sections. (From Andersen 1983.)

57

ment of water by PEG over a period which may take a year or more. Freeze-drying is another technique with a good record for the treatment of small wood artifacts, basketry and textiles; the water is converted and extracted as vapour under vacuum at low temperatures. At the moment, if anti-shrink efficiency (ASE) is taken as a general guide for results, freeze-drying from PEG400 solutions at 25–30% concentrations, or bulking of the wood with PEG540 blend over a long period, or bulking with PEG4000 using tertiary-butanol as solvent to promote penetration, appear to be among the best methods for wood (Grattan 1982b; Schwein-gruber 1982; Oddy 1975).

Where many hand-held implements have been recovered, or where wooden bowls have been used for oil or fat, considerable problems have been found in conservation; hardwood paddles, for example, exhibit variable checking (transverse and longitudinal cracking) at the tops and in the lower part of the handles, where they were gripped tightly by the users' hands (Gleeson and Grosso 1976), and the same is probably true of other implements such as axe handles and bows (figure 36). But the conservation of the whole range of wetland materials involves a number of different techniques, and collaboration between archaeologists and conservators is essential. With the rapid growth of interest in wetland sites, the enormous quantities of wooden artifacts both structural and instrumental are already posing problems. How much to save intact, how much to sacrifice for analyses, and how much to discard, may well be one major problem to be debated in the near future. Here a careful sampling strategy has to be imposed, just as it must be for other wetland aspects of an ecological nature.

Figure 36. Mesolithic bow from Tybrind Vig, Denmark. Artifacts such as these occasionally create problems in conservation through differential degrees of oil spread into the wood at handles or grips. (From Andersen 1980.)

ECOLOGICAL EVIDENCE. One of the attractions of wetland sites is the abundance of evidence about past environments that will be preserved as beetle, molluscan and other invertebrate remains; and pollen, wood, leaves, and seeds, and fungi and other microscopic and macroscopic fragments (e.g. figure 37). Each of these is a specialist subject not only in the study but in the actual extraction from the site. Sampling of a wetland site is always a complex business and by rights should be undertaken by the specialists concerned who will advise on precise locations and quantities of samples to be collected. Failing their attendance, the archaeologist must have adequate instruction on sampling for environmental data, must avoid contamination of samples, and must take samples for specific reasons. Among these will be questions of general climatic episodes, local environmental conditions, chronology, human alteration of the landscape, economic and dietary practices, and cultural behaviour on site. Some of these are obvious problems, others will be less so, and often a general environmental sampling programme will yield very specific and rewarding information.

Sediments. There are numerous and increasingly varied analyses which can now be made on wetland samples. Sediments themselves, such as clays and silts, are useful indicators of past environmental events. At the Neolithic settlement of Twann, in the Lake of Bienne, Switzerland, for instance, sediment studies have been extensively employed (Furger *et al.* 1977, 1981). Sediment grain size and identification of their mineral and rock origins, with clay particle analysis, organic component identification, and major rock characterisation, have allowed some conclusions to be drawn about the sedimentological processes of both human and natural agencies on the site. Granulometric studies and diatom analyses can often provide precise information about the natural agencies at work in the formation of such deposits (general assessment, Evans 1978). Diatoms are unicellular algae which occupy many wet deposits; as their cell walls are of silica, survival can be good in waterlogged conditions. There are many different species, indicative of various habitats, which can thus provide useful environmental information. At Twann, studies of carbon, humus and phosphate contents, and pH levels, permit further thoughts on lake level alterations, and human activities, on and near the site. All of these studies, allied to stratigraphical observations, tree-ring dating and other factors, allow a dynamic model of settlement activities to be proposed;

59

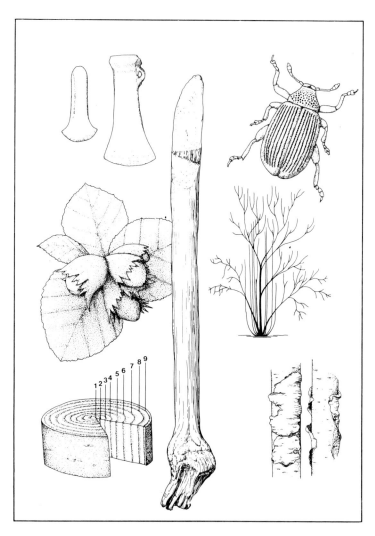

Figure 37. Representation of studies in a single piece of round wood from an archaeo-logical site. The sharpening facets may allow identification of the tool type, or even a particular tool with damaged blade. The wood identification, tree-ring counts, beetle and fungus infestation, and rod size and butt configuration can provide information about the environment and human influences upon it. (Drawn by S. Rouillard.)

60

25 occupations occurred on the site, with 21 desertions necessitated by rising lake levels (a good example of stubbornness if nothing else), and 2 disasters by fire. This is the detail required by archaeologists in their efforts to understand how societies operated in the past, and the point must be that a wide range of different kinds of evidence is required.

Molluscs and beetles. Freshwater molluscs have been a rather neglected field of enquiry on wetland sites, but they too can yield valuable evidence. Various species prefer slow-moving streams rich in plants, others live in well-oxygenated water such as rivers, and a third diagnostic group prefer poorly-aerated still waters which may dry out completely from time to time. Thus a stratigraphical series of freshwater molluscan remains could demonstrate variations in the intensity of one or more of these conditions, and this could have implications for site location as well as likely conservation problems. Many freshwater molluscs, however, are catholic in their environmental preferences and are therefore of little use for these purposes.

Remains of beetles can provide precise data about temperature, shade, moisture and plant communities (Girling 1984). As an example, a species *Rhysocles sulcatus* from Neolithic peat in Somerset is found only in mature undisturbed forest, and is extinct in Britain today, but it indicates this type of woodland in the fourth millennium B C in south-west England. Soft-bodied animals such as spiders may also be preserved in soft wet peat, and some may be very specific in environmental terms; *Dolomedes,* the raft spider, is a hunter on the surface of standing or slow-moving water and its presence in Neolithic Somerset swamp peat is appropriate. Fly pupae from cattle stalling in the Neolithic settlement at Twann, Switzerland, also indicate particular conditions of warmth and wetness (Guyan 1981).

Pollen and plants. More common are studies of plants from wetlands, and these include wood, bark, leaves and seeds. As in dryland archaeology, pollen will generally form a basic study for regional environmental conditions and for the establishment of a general chronological sequence, through the identification of pollen zones characterised by certain groups of plants, such as a zone of oak mixed forest, or birch-pine, or a phase when elm and perhaps other major trees decline abruptly (e.g. for the Sweet Track, England: Caseldine 1984 ; Switzerland: Troels-Smith 1981). Pollen analysis is a specialist study under the microscope, and its results can be very precise. At the Neolithic settlement of Charavines, France, analyses of pollen cores have identified two clear episodes of forest clearance, one when the first settlers arrived on the lakeshore and began felling the pine, beech and oak, then planting the fertile soils with wheat and other crops. After a short period of 20–30 years, the settlement was abandoned and the forest began to re-assert itself until the land was once again tree-covered. This period lasted 30–40 years, and then again human interference began with widespread felling of trees, and planting of wheat, barley and flax. This second major occupation, 20–30 years long, was ended when rising lake waters drowned the site. The interpretation of the pollen at Charavines depends on other factors, of course, and among these are studies of invertebrates, macroscopic plant remains and tree-ring analyses (Bocquet 1982).

Macroscopic plant remains are also useful indicators, but rather than regional patterns they will reflect conditions at or near the sampling site itself. Leaves, bark and twigs, and associated animal life such as beetles or fungi which may have inhabited parts of plants, give a combined environmental picture fortified by their complementary evidence. An organic deposit such as peat, or waterlogged silt or muck which has a high organic content, will contain large quantities of identifiable plant remains as well as pollen and other particles suitable for microscopic studies. A coarsely-textured peat will break along planes of deposition and reveal, for example, birch leaves, twigs, bog beans, mosses and other plant remains barely disintegrated (figure 38); a humified dark peat, however, will be consolidated and few plants will be readily identifiable except perhaps heather stems. Where lake silts are involved, large quantities of plant remains may well be preserved, and the residues from crop-processing methods may survive as well as elements of flooring, bedding, even bouquets of flowers.

At Charavines, a wide range of wild nuts, berries and fruits (e.g. hazelnuts, strawberries, apples) attest not only to the food requirements or preferences of the Neolithic settlers, but also to the environmental conditions which permitted such plants to flourish within the site territory. At the Glastonbury Iron Age village in England, the conditions for the preservation of macroscopic plant remains were excellent, and a wide range of wild plants including sloe-, elder- and blackberries was identified. Plant materials can also be culturally distinctive; at Glastonbury, reed for thatch, and withies for basketry,

62

Figure 38. Layering in raised bog peat, Somerset Levels, England. The less humified lighter more fibrous layers are clearly distinguished from the more humified darker layers, representing different conditions of plant deposition and decay.

were preserved, and from Charavines there were traces of wool and flax from woven textiles and rope. The Swiss lakeside settlements have yielded huge quantities of such materials, and present a detailed picture of the multifarious activities carried out by Neolithic and Bronze Age societies (Heitz, Jacomet and Zoller 1981).

The retrieval of such evidence involves careful selection of samples, and various procedures of sieving and floating of the deposits in water or with added separation agents. This is not the place for a detailed exposition of sieving and floating methods, but simple water-based separation is often a first treatment for deposits, using screening of various mesh sizes with water spraying or water swirls beneath, in order to separate plant residues from other materials. Chemical flotation, using calgon or hydrogen peroxide, may often be required, and may be succeeded by other solutions to float seeds, fish scales, and bark, and to extract other components. The problem with such methods is that other evidence, such as fungal remains, may well be destroyed by the techniques of extraction, and there is much room for experimentation in this field of enquiry. The use of froth flotation and

63

other air-bubble machines for bulk processing of wetland deposits is currently another field for experiment, due to disputes about the efficiency rates for these machines.

Wood. A separate but important specialist study on wetland sites is concerned with the wood itself. Information on forest species (figure 39), the nature of ancient woodlands, the development of wood management by coppicing practices, as well as woodworking technologies, is readily available on well-preserved wetland sites (Schweingruber 1976; Stotzer *et al.* 1976). Where an abundance of wood has survived, wood-working techniques can be examined in great detail (figure 40), from felling, splitting into planks, working of edges or ends, to driving pegs or placing timber on site in structures (Orme and Coles 1983). Each activity will leave characteristic traces, and sometimes individual axes can be identified by the ridges left behind on the facets of the wood. This has been done at Alvastra, Sweden (Malmer 1978), and on Neolithic and Bronze Age tracks in Somerset. In terms of wooden equipment, the variety seems endless, and many new types of artifacts have been found on waterlogged sites (e.g. wheels and carts, Hayen 1973; vessels, Capelle 1983; bows, Clark 1963; baskets, Bernick 1983; masks and figures, Purdy 1982; spoons, Müller-Beck 1965).

Where roundwood has survived, with bark still attached, studies of woodland management practices can be attempted. The characteristic heels of coppiced hazel rods in the Walton Heath hurdles from Somerset, associated with long straight rods and poles, of variable ages, indicate some form of draw-felling (i.e. selective felling for diameter uniformity) in hazel woodland some distance away from the marsh in which the hurdles eventually came to rest (Rackham 1977).

In addition to these studies of wood, tree-ring analysis and dendrochronology can permit very precise chronologies to be worked out through cross-matching tree-rings from the site to known dated tree-ring sequences; some of the lakeside settlements in Switzerland can be dated to actual years B C through comparison with a complete sequence back from the present day (Ruoff 1981c; Arnold 1983). A welter of posts and timbers from collapsed prehistoric structures can be analysed into sets of patterns through cross-matching of individual pieces, and the life of a settlement can be measured in individual years, rather than decades or even centuries (e.g. Wyss 1976). Where a long-lived settlement is represented by many piles and posts of oak or other woods,

64

SITE: SWQV

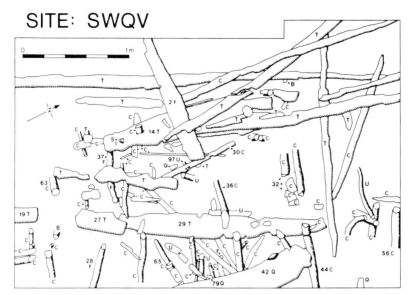

Figure 39. Plan of a small part of the Sweet Track, Somerset, England, to show the mass of round wood and timber from two more-or-less contemporary structures. This is a standard publication plan, with numbered pieces for tree-ring discussion, and all pieces identified for wood species: T Tilia (lime); F Fraxinus (ash); C Corylus (hazel); B Betula (birch); U Ulmus (elm); Q Quercus (oak); I Ilex (holly). (From Somerset Levels Papers 10, 1984.)
Figure 40. Facets left by stone axe on roundwood pegs from the Sweet Track, Somerset, England. The pegs, buried in peat for c. 6000 years, are perfectly preserved in terms of shape, but are severely degraded in cell structure through excessive waterlogging.

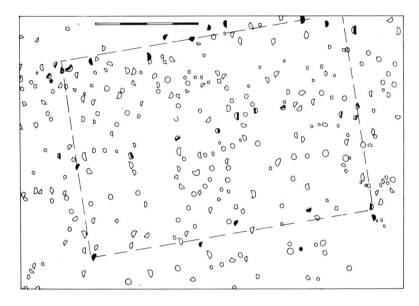

found in bewildering quantities and seemingly at random, tree-ring studies can allow each structure to be identified by relating each pile to one another and finding those which form an exact contemporary group (e.g. Bartholin 1978; see figure 41). Equivalent detail is available in the establishment of an internal chronology for wooden trackways such as the Sweet Track in England where individual planks from different parts of the structure, over 1800 m long, can be identified to particular trees which supplied radial, trimmed radial and even tangential planks (Morgan 1984; figure 42).

If adequate quantities of tree-ring samples are available, then selected sets of annual growth rings can be extracted for radiocarbon dating, and this is how the latter is correlated with absolute chronological years. For normal radiocarbon dating of a site or deposit, small young branches or other young plants are the best possible source. Most wetlands themselves are eminently suitable for radiocarbon dating; a peatbog is nothing but an organic deposit any part of which can be selected for dating (Orme 1982). The avoidance of charcoal or fragments of potentially very old timber for dating by radiocarbon analysis helps to clarify chronology rather than unnecessarily complicate it.

66

OAK plank end years

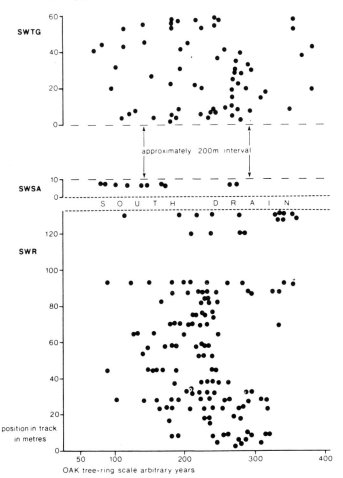

Figure 41 (facing). Plan of a Late Bronze Age structure at Auvernier, Switzerland, extracted from vertical piles by tree-ring analysis. The solid sections are posts cut within a 3-year period c. 3000 years ago, the half-solid probably also of this episode. Open sections are not of this period. The house is c. 10 m long. (From Strahm 1976.)

Figure 42 (above). Oak planks from the Sweet Track. The diagram shows how different oaks were treated along the northern part of the 1800 m structure. Three sites are shown, SWR, SWSA and SWTG, representing c. 400 m of the track (including a gap of 200 m). Each dot represents the end year of an oak plank, the maximum age being c. 400 years. (From Morgan 1984.)

67

COST If all of these studies suggest a very large investment of time, facilities, expertise and therefore money to excavate a wetland site, that is exactly right. Wetland sites are fragile yet richly rewarding, and they cost far more to investigate than do dryland sites (Ruoff 1981a; Macdonald 1982). Wetland sites are slower to dig, and vastly slower to analyse even if only a basic sampling strategy is adopted for environmental studies. It is extremely difficult to estimate this in terms of time and money, but as a general guide, or invitation to argument, a wetland site may be 3–10 times as slow to dig, conserve and study as a dryland site, and therefore will be at least 5 times more expensive in the final reckoning, with all of the many specialist studies included. A proper wetland study will involve not only archaeologists and their usual pre- and post-excavation specialists for geology, pollen, molluscs, pottery, bone, flint etc., but *also* experts in the study of plant remains, beetles, fungi, diatoms, sediments, tree-rings, wood technology and woodlands, textiles and hides, and doubtless others, among whom conservators will bulk large.

The need for an extremely rigorous sampling strategy will be obvious. The yield of evidence, most of which will require specialist treatment and analysis, is likely to be so great that one month's excavation, for example, may require several years of post-excavation work by a variety of specialists. Without provision for such work, wetland excavations are of little value.

The real value of a wetland site is in its exposure of totally new kinds of evidence about environment, economy and other cultural behaviour. To undertake wetland archaeology involves a conviction that its greater expense is worth the greater yield of information. Not to adopt this approach is to doom archaeology to a continued accumulation of the limited kinds of information whch we have been collecting for decades. This information is valuable, of course, but it is surely time to move now to new kinds of evidence to allow us to develop a greater and more reliable understanding of past human behaviour.

In all of this it is assumed that excavation equals total destruction. The responsibility for publication of the results of wetland sites is in fact even greater than for dryland sites. Wetland sites are unusual and expensive and we cannot afford to spend resources on them if their information remains unavailable for the public and for the archive of information about the past.

68

3

Sites and their landscapes

Modern archaeological practice is concerned with sites in their landscape, in the processes that led to site formation, and in the behavioural patterns represented and discernible on the site. Wetland sites
should be capable of incorporation in such concepts, but in not all cases
has the full potential been achieved. Any well-preserved wetland site is
likely to yield such an abundance of artifacts and economic data that it
stands almost alone as a guide and inspiration for future work. Such a
site was Star Carr, a Mesolithic hunting and gathering station in
Yorkshire (Clark 1954); the excavation and publication of this site was
a landmark both for Mesolithic studies and for wetland archaeology.
Comparable Mesolithic sites such as Nizhneyo Veretye in the Lacha
basin, USSR (Oshibkina 1982), and Tybrind Vig, Denmark, have
already begun to reveal the wealth and abundance of organic material
on a well-preserved settlement; the Russian site lies beneath peat, the
Danish beneath water, and both pick out the obvious Mesolithic
omissions from a dryland site (wooden bows and arrowshafts for the
ubiquitous flint arrowheads, shafts and handles for stone axes and
adzes). They also reveal unexpected facets of Mesolithic equipment,
such as elaborately decorated wooden artifacts (figure 43) as well as
unique evidence about the environment and economy of these sites.

The discovery and excavation of the site at Tybrind Vig, Denmark,
has been noted, and its importance to Mesolithic studies in north and
western Europe can perhaps be gauged by a brief description of the
artifacts alone, without the detailed environmental picture now constructed for the site (Andersen 1980, 1983). The site lay originally on a
peninsula in a small bay, and the inhabitants of c. 4000–3700 BC were
primarily concerned with fishing, as well as hunting and gathering
inland from the coast. Some of the pottery recovered bore traces of fish
soup probably made from cod with wild grass flavouring. Along with a
wide range of flint, stone, bone and antler tools, were wooden bows
and arrows, spears and stakes, axe handles and digging sticks, leister

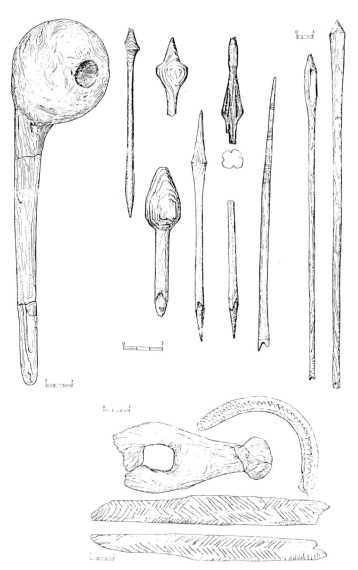

Figure 43. Mesolithic artifacts from Nizhneyo Veretye, Lacha basin, USSR, c. 7th millennium BC. The pine arrow foreshafts would be attached to the shaft by string or resin. Blunt-ended points are probably for birds or small fur-bearing animals. One has slots for flint inserts, but all others require no inorganic parts and would thus leave no trace of their existence on a dry site. The knobbed pieces are axe hafts, made of rootwork with perforation for a stone or horn blade. The carved and decorated wooden pieces are less easy to identify for function. (From Oshibkina 1982.)

prongs, clubs and other artifacts as well as lines of hazel rods set up as fish traps just off-shore from the settlement. A lime-trunk dugout 10 m long was associated with the camp, and the size of the tree and its clear texture is indicative of a virgin forest with high canopy trees. Wooden paddles of ash (figure 44) include two with imprinted and painted designs on the blades (figure 45); these are unique, and the first decorated wooden artifacts from the European Mesolithic. The site provides a salutary reminder to archaeologists that almost all of the Mesolithic studies so far conducted in Europe are concerned with flint tools, sparsely represented at Tybrind Vig, and thus may be concerned with only a fraction of the evidence, and unrepresentative at that. Wetland sites can set the inorganic component of prehistoric and early historic material culture in perspective, and unveil entirely new types of evidence.

This point does not need elaborating, but just as Mesolithic studies in northern Europe are being greatly advanced by wetland sites, so the process of understanding about prehistoric Australian inhabitants is changing through wetland discoveries. At Wyrie swamp, in south Australia, an occupation c. 10000–9000 years ago left debris consisting of chert tools and wooden implements, including the earliest known examples of what seem to be boomerangs, made of Drooping Sheoak, a tree still growing in the swamp (Luebbers 1975). Kangaroo butchery sites (Crowley 1981) and aboriginal burial complexes on wetland margins and levees (Thorne and Macumber 1972), also begin to redress the imbalance of evidence about early inhabitants, and reduce the importance of stone tools as cultural markers.

Nonetheless, it is in the opportunity for landscape archaeology, sites in their setting, that wetlands offer their greatest potential, and a brief survey of some current projects will document this. From the beginning of wetland archaeology, the lakeside settlements in Alpine Europe (in Switzerland, France and Italy in particular) have been dominant. As we have seen, in recent years developments along the lake shores have permitted new excavations to be undertaken and new studies to be initiated. One of the settlements, at Auvernier (figure 46), now has a detailed history beginning in 807 BC, with major alterations occurring during occupation in 796–787 BC, and partial abandonment, followed by rebuilding, in 783–779 BC. The processes of cultural behaviour, exemplified by associated studies of plant and

71

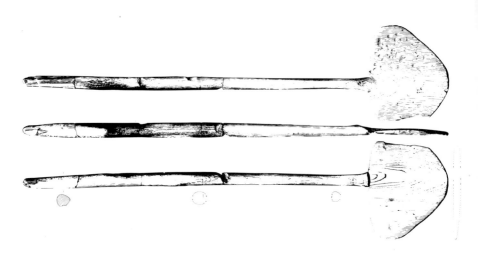

Figure 44. Ashwood paddle from Tybrind Vig, Denmark, made from a single piece of wood split and carved into shape. Differential wear in the handle, at top and near the base, and absence of worn segments on the blade itself, indicate the use for water propulsion rather than as digging tool or reed cutter. (From Andersen 1980.)

Figure 45. One of two decorated wooden paddles from Tybrind Vig, Denmark. The design is imprinted, probably by delicate hammering or pressure and then painted in brown ochre-based paint. The existence of such Mesolithic art on wood is otherwise unknown in north-western Europe. (From Andersen 1980.)

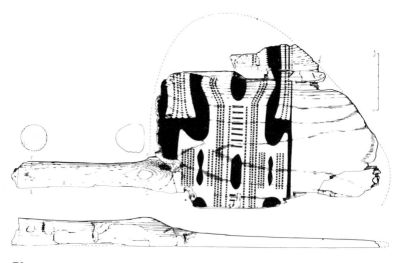

72

animal remains, and inorganic domestic equipment, are only now under way, but clearly the chronological precision from tree-ring evidence will permit a dynamic model of behaviour to be advanced. In addition, as most of the nineteenth-century excavations at Auvernier did not distinguish between thin yet discrete layers on these early sites, the value of the current work will extend well beyond the actual sites themselves (Arnold 1983; Strahm 1976; Egloff 1977).

In Lake Zürich (figure 47), a major series of excavations is also under way, with Neolithic and Bronze Age settlements yielding multiple layers of occupation, separable in detail only by tree-ring analysis, and huge quantities of material including hundreds of organic and inorganic artifacts, house platforms and foundations, and whole village streets identifiable. The full study and publication will occupy many years (Ruoff 1981a; Heitz *et al.* 1981; Ruoff 1981b; Höneisen 1982), yet the yield of information will surely warrant such expense. The Neolithic hamlet of Egolzwil in Switzerland has now been pub-

Figure 46. A reconstruction of the 8th c. BC settlement at Auvernier, Switzerland, based on archaeological studies on the site, and environmental studies of the sediments and plant remains from the immediate area. The site is enclosed in part on the open shore. The reconstruction as a lake-side settlement is in contrast to previous views that many of the settlements were defended and set on piles within the lakes. (From Arnold 1983.)

73

lished in part and the settlement identified as consisting of seven buildings (figure 48), built of alder hurdles, as well as oak, birch and poplar, roofed by reeds, and occupied by 7 families of perhaps 35 people (8 women, 11 men and 16 children were found in a contemporary cemetery nearby; who buried the last of them is unanswered!). The first hamlet was extended after only 6 years, when 2 more buildings were erected, and the others repaired. As the buildings lay upon unstable ground, their hearths sank and were rebuilt on a number of occasions. After another 6 years, the site was abandoned, probably because of a rising water-table, and it was soon overwhelmed by water. Although animal bones were not abundant, due to scavengers, a preponderance were of cattle. Pollen and other plant remains indicate cleared woodland, with cereal cultivation nearby, and with fruits, nuts and other plants used for food or flooring of bedding. This site and its precisely identifiable components is not exceptional for such lakeside settlements (Wyss 1976).

Work on similar sites in Alpine France and Italy is also under way. At Charavines on Lake Paladru, tree-ring studies permit the development of a Neolithic settlement to be identified to within single years, with timber seasoned for one year before house building, a second house built one year later, rebuilding of the first after 7 years, rebuilding of both after another 9 years, and abandonment after a further period of 12–15 years (Bocquet 1982). As the lake silts covered the site soon after its final abandonment, the thousands of artifacts left behind were not subject to displacement by wind or water, and so elaborate reconstructions of varieties of economic and other cultural activities can be attempted, through both distributions and analyses of use-wear traces. Pots can be re-assembled from sherds found in groups, and identified as breaking and abandoned inside particular buildings, or sometimes outside buildings. Dismemberment of both wild and domestic animals took place outside the houses, and some weaving of wool and flax as well. Among the abundant remains of tools, weapons, and other artifacts, stone axes set in antler sleeves and flint daggers and sickles still with their handles and hafts remind us of what would remain behind if this were a dryland site. Basketry and pottery vessels were common over much of the settlement, and some traces of food residues survive. Hunting by bow and arrow was a major concern, as interpreted both by weapons and by wild animal

74

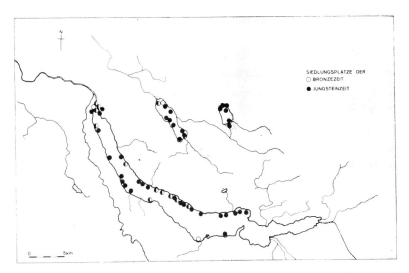

Figure 47. Map of Neolithic and Late Bronze Age lakeside settlements in the Lakes of Zurich and showing the great number of Neolithic sites preserved by rising lake levels. Gaps in the archaeological record, e.g. in the 2nd millennium BC, presumably mean that lake levels were very high and settlements were set well inland and thus not preserved as well as these earlier and later ones sealed by water. (From Ruoff 1981.)

Figure 48. Part of the excavation plans of the Neolithic settlement at Egolzwil, Switzerland, showing the rebuilt hearth areas of four houses, with (schematic) house outlines established by tree-ring analysis and fence line similarly identified to the north. The grid lines are 1 m. (From Wyss 1976.)

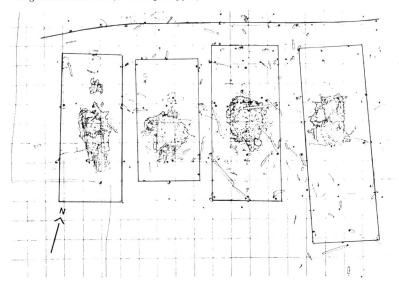

remains, which outnumber those of domestic animals. Dugout canoes on the lake were presumably used for fishing and communication. Wooden spoons, needles and weaving combs, and fragments of baked bread loaves, a half-eaten apple and other food remains have been recovered (Lundstrom-Baudais 1984).

From northern Italy, at Fiavè and Lavagnone, Bronze Age settlements set beside small lakes are currently being studied, with particular attention being given to platform and house structures (Perini 1976; 1983) (figure 49). A variety of improvisations has been identified, with some buildings set on piles within the water, others on the shores. Here, the great depth of peat and silt which came to cover the sites has resulted in the preservation of quite unusual lengths of vertical posts and piles. The quantity of long straight trees chosen for the massive constructions tell us much about the forests surrounding the lakes and marshes (figure 50).

The evidence derived from long periods of investigation allows the development of archaeological models which help to explain the persistence and the variety of prehistoric settlement patterns in and around the Alpine lakes. Site catchment-analysis can be used to demonstrate the range of terrain suitable for exploitation in the second millennium BC, and this has long been an attractive – if unnamed – approach to such types of settlement wherever they occur (e.g. Coles 1976; Bocquet 1982; Bernick 1983; Arnold 1983).

Wetland archaeological work on such a scale is not often possible due to its cost, but there can be no doubt that many other wetland sites could yield equally important evidence for their own regions. In Scotland, for example, the current work on crannogs, some now landlocked, others still off-shore, yet others now deeply submerged beneath flooded valley reservoirs, should change our conception about small settlements of the fifth century BC–seventeenth century AD in northern Britain (Morrison 1980).

In Florida, wetland archaeology has been revived after a disastrous

Figure 49. Bronze Age settlement at Fiavè, Italy, with multiple wooden piles set between pairs of transverse logs held together as a rigid frame. Date c. 14th century BC. (From Perini 1983.)

Figure 50. Top parts of long wooden piles, 16th-15th c. BC, Fiavè, Italy. The notches for attachment of the horizontal framing which held the houses permit accurate reconstructions of the settlement. (From Perini 1983.)

76

period of neglect following Cushing's work at Key Marco. Through persistent survey, the claim can now be made that 'Organic artifacts in Florida are known to be more abundant than anywhere in the world at the present time, including the largest number of prehistoric watercraft' (Purdy 1982) (figure 51). Among these artifacts are totems, figurines, masks and other unusual reflections of cult practices, not normally encountered on ancient sites. Some of these wooden artifacts date from the fifth millennium BC, and many others belong to the period when Europeans first penetrated the region. At Little Salt Springs, a sinkhole or swamp was used for burial in the late fifth and early fourth millennium BC. Conditions for the preservation of the bodies were exceptional, so that the excavators could write 'The bodies were buried . . . either on biers of green leafy limbs of wax myrtle or with leafy limbs placed between the arms and torso. Portions of the body were ceremonially wrapped with grass' (quoted in Macdonald and Purdy 1982). In the Okeechobee basin, settlers of the early first millennium BC constructed earthworks above the levels of the floodwaters for maize cultivation; later, two of these earthworks became focal points for burial preparations, and a wooden platform was built over an adjacent artificial pond to serve as a bier for up to 300 bundled burials (figure 52). The platform was partly supported by pine logs carved with bird and other animal heads, and was decorated around its edge by carved totemic symbols on wooden posts, depicting the eagle, otter, turkey, owl, bobcat, duck and other waterbirds. In time, the platform was burned and collapsed into the pond to await its discovery (Sears 1982). These are only two examples of the unique kinds of evidence which can come from the Florida wetlands, and which are currently being destroyed.

Unlike the exploration of Alpine lakeside sites, however, modern wetland archaeology in Florida is still not well-established. The peat deposits in Florida cover 3 million acres (1.2 million ha) much of which is now being drained. The loss can be dramatic; in the northern Everglades flow area, drainage over the past 70 years has caused peat losses, due to biochemical degradation, of over 50% in places. In south Florida, shrinkage losses of 1.5 m of muck have occurred in the past 50 years in areas affected by adjacent drainage schemes. With these go the destruction of countless artifacts of historic and prehistoric importance. After a century of occasional but persistent recovery of pre-

78

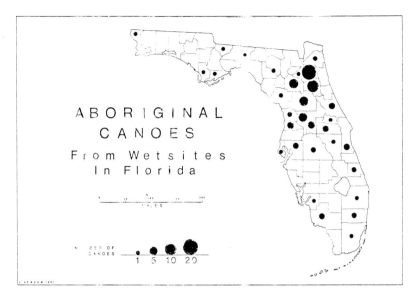

Figure 51. Distribution of log boats from wet sites in Florida, USA, quantified by counties and based on surveys by B. Purdy. The number of these boats, over 100, exceeds that from other comparable wetland areas of the world, but doubtless other surveys would considerably augment the record of watercraft. (From Purdy 1982.)

historic wooden artifacts from waterlogged sites, there had not been a single archaeological survey of wetlands until 1980 (Purdy 1982). Almost all of the organic finds were recovered during drainage operations, few through archaeological excavations; the conservation of the objects was totally inadequate, and most of the known sites were destroyed before any proper examination could be made. This area is not unique for the general lack of interest taken in the archaeology of its wetlands, but there can be few countries with any respect for the past which have done as little as was done at a site near Bay West, Florida. Here, a cypress pond was being dredged, and about 500 pieces of prehistoric worked wood were recovered by amateur archaeologists, almost all from spoil heaps as the dredger pulled peat, muck and ancient relics from the pond; the date of this operation was 1980, not 1880.

79

Figure 52. Reconstruction of burial practices in the Okeechobee Basin, Florida, USA, 1st millennium BC. A wooden platform was built over a pond, and bundled burials were stored and marked by carved wooden symbols, perhaps totemic. The site eventually collapsed into the pond. (From Macdonald and Purdy 1982.)

80

On the western coast of North America, wetland archaeology has been practised for many years, but little has yet been published from a number of important sites. The environment of the coastal region is such that middens and fishing stations, as well as major settlements, are abundant in locations where mud-slides or river alterations can protect or expose them, and a number of such sites are now known (Croes 1976a). At many sites, including Little Qualicum and Lachane, evidence dating from 2000 BC to AD 1500 has been recovered, among which are large quantities of organic artifacts. These sites demonstrate a long continuity of woodworking and basketry technologies, and of subsistence economies based on the rich resources of the land and sea. Comparison with the ·historically-documented native communities makes this a particularly fruitful area for wetland studies.

The Lachane site in Prince Rupert, British Columbia, is one of many wet sites that exist along the coast (Inglis 1976). Rainfall in this particular northern area is over 1 m per year, and many streams drain from the mountains immediately inland. The prehistoric communities occupying the region tended in many cases to build their wooden houses with floors directly over flowing streams, and debris from such occupations can be waterlogged and preserved by midden accumulation or mudslides. The Lachane site appears to have been just such a midden, located between two houses; it was damaged by railway construction c. 1900, by gun emplacements and a road c. 1940, by house building c. 1950, then totally destroyed by harbour construction in 1973. Rescue excavations discovered traces of forest clearance for the original occupation of about 2000 years ago, and an abundance of artifacts from the subsequent settlements. Many of these were broken, or were pieces in the process of manufacture, discarded in the stream. There were many wooden shafts, points, wedges, digging sticks, paddle fragments and boxes, as well as basketry elements. Conditions for preservation of woodworking details were particularly good (figure 25); the wedges, for example, were of fir, some of them of compression wood (at tree-trunk and branch intersection where cells are compressed and the wood is more solid) and some with four-strand collars of red cedar root. The boxes were of bentwood red cedar, kerfed in three corners with the fourth L-slotted and stitched with cordage, and base attached by pitch; birchbark trays had slat reinforcement of the edges and were sewn with cedar bark.

81

The Little Qualicum River site, on the east coast of Vancouver Island, is one of the very few wet sites published in full (Bernick 1983). This was a salmon fishing station on a small bay in the left bank of the river as it approached the Strait of Georgia. The occupation itself, of about 1000 A D, was on dry land, but debris disposal took place on the river edge (figure 53), and the fishing activities also left much material in waterlogged conditions; the site may have been of the same character as Tybrind Vig. Chum salmon were caught by a tidal weir made of latticework 'woven' with cedar bark and Douglas fir, lashed to a stake frame. Nets and basketry fragments, with cord-tied stone anchors, wooden fishhooks, and bark bailers, indicate other fishing methods. Enough pieces remained to suggest that the fish were smoked for storage and later consumption, or for exchange with groups from the interior. The site yielded only 63 stone artifacts, over 100 bone and antler tools, and many fragments of wood and bark basketry, matting, cordage, bracelets, wedges, points, most of red cedar (*Thuja plicata*). Animal remains consisted of deer, dog, with a few seal and elk, water birds, fish and clam, and a very detailed environmental and cultural assessment could be advanced on the basis of excellent preservation as well as ethnographic evidence for the Coast Salish people.

Wetland survey of an intensive kind is under way in the 1 million acres (400000 ha) of peats and silts in the Fenlands of eastern England. Drainage of parts of this huge area has been carried out for centuries, and peat shrinkage due to desiccation and erosion has been very great. However, current wetland archaeology in the Fenlands has succeeded beyond expectation in the discovery of hundreds of sites hitherto unknown (Hall 1981). Burial mounds, some standing on a Bronze Age dryland surface and subsequently drowned by flooding and submerged by peat formation, now begin to appear above the surface of the shrinking peatland; totally undamaged by the plough, the cemeteries of barrows are fully complete, and offer opportunities for preservation policies or excavation programme. By judicious identification of major flooding episodes, and their effect on local topography, landscapes of the Neolithic, Bronze and Iron Ages, and later periods, can be re-created, and the human resource use of the land and water more fully understood (figure 16–17).

At the present time, field survey is a major priority for the Fenlands,

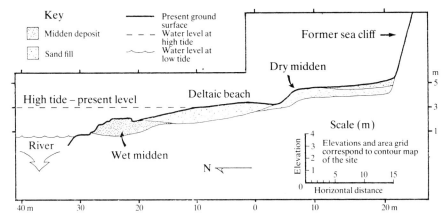

Figure 53. A section through the Little Qualicum River site, British Columbia, Canada. The settlement was based upslope on a dry area and fishing took place at river's *edge where a midden was created. Rising water levels drowned the fishing station and deposited beach sands and gravels upon the upper midden edge. (From Bernick 1983.)

but excavations in advance of massive dewatering schemes are also in hand. A Neolithic causewayed enclosure at Etton, Cambs, has water-logged ditches with organic material well preserved (Pryor and Kinnes 1982) (figure 28). A first millennium BC wooden platform at Flag Fen, Cambs (cf. figure 49), only found through persistent ditch surveys over a wide area (Pryor 1983), may be only one of many such structures still to be discovered. At Fiskerton, Lincs, a causeway or jetty on the River Witham points to an interest in river and fen products, as well as in river traffic, in the Iron Age (Field n.d.). The Fenland work as a whole, combining survey, excavation and environmental investigations, is probably the most important wetland development in British archaeology. The threats from drainage to the uppermost deposits are persistent and increasing, and the same may be said for other landscape surveys, such as those in the Rhine-Meuse delta of the Netherlands, in areas of northern Britain, in the Florida wetlands and in the Australian marshlands.

Buried landscapes are sometimes revealed by peat-cutting, often disastrously, as machine removal of peat rapidly destroys large areas and horizons. One such is the central Irish bogland, of 3 million acres (1.2 million ha), parts of which have been cut for burning for centuries. During the major period of hand-cutting (c. 1830–1930), many pre-

83

historic and early historic discoveries were made, and about 60% of the holdings in the National Museum of Ireland come from the peatlands of Ireland, both raised bog and blanket bog. Many of these artifacts are organic, wooden shields (figure 54), tubs, wheels, tools and weapons, and textiles and leather, but there are also quantities of metal objects of bronze and gold. Today, large parts of the central Irish wetland are being drained and quarried for electricity production through Bord na Móna, and a measure of the exercise is the extraction of 5 million tonnes of peat in 1981–2 (Hammond 1981; Bord na Móna 1981–2). Within 40 years or so all the usable peat will be gone, and with it a vast amount of evidence about early Irish society. In other areas, however, hand-cutting of peat can permit the gradual uncovering of prehistoric structures, and lead to field survey to trace still-buried monuments. In Co. Mayo, Ireland, just such a programme of work is underway, with local peat-cutting gradually exposing a Neolithic land surface at Behy-Glenulra, which contains stone fences, houses and tombs in predictable patterns, a unique opportunity to see a complete landscape (Caulfield 1983). Blanket bog formation in the third and second millennia BC completely covered the Neolithic settlements, fields and cemeteries, and although conditions for the preservation of organic material are not at all good, the actual physical configuration and organisation of the land is preserved (figure 55). This is a comparable phenomenon to the preservation of Bronze Age settlements and field systems on Dartmoor and many other moors of Britain. Although the organic elements of the occupations are not well preserved, there are still unusual opportunities here for landscape archaeology through the sealing of ancient landscapes by wetland development. The blanket bog surveys and other smaller-scale work in Ireland only hint at the possibilities for raised bog studies. It would be well to remember the expense of archaeological work in wetlands, but also to reflect on the unique evidence that would be gained by such work. Field survey and excavation would be guaranteed a yield of information that would complement data obtained from current dryland archaeology in Ireland. The same could be said for the Florida wetlands, and in a similar manner for the small boglands of northern England and Scotland, where known archaeological organic sites have been lost through inattention.

Figure 54. Leather shield of the first millennium BC from Clonbrin, Co. Longford; wooden mould for the shaping of leather shields from Churchfield, Co. Mayo. Both found during peat-cutting. (Photos Nat. Mus. Ireland.)

Figure 55. Plan of a Neolithic landscape at Behy-Glenulra, Co. Mayo, Ireland. The field boundaries and enclosures are of stone, the whole preserved by the development of blanket bog in the entire area. The shaded area is uncut bog still covering parts of the landscape of the 3rd millennium BC. (From Caulfield 1982.)

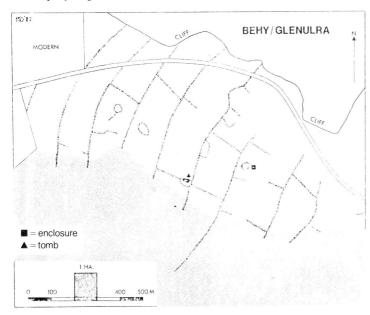

In the north German lowlands there were formerly large expanses of peat, making up about a quarter of the total land of Lower Saxony, and a comparable area of Schleswig-Holstein. For centuries the peat has been drained and cut for fuel and fertiliser, and today only a few pockets of the original peatbog remain (Hayen 1980; Eigner 1978). Some are now nature reserves and are protected, others are being partly cut and will then be conserved as relics, but a majority will be destroyed. The marshlands were occupied from about 4000 BC and many wooden roads and tracks were built into and across the wet areas (figure 56); this activity continued well into the Middle Ages, and about 300 of these trackways are now known to have existed. Some were heavy logroads, others slender footpaths, and a few are as much as 10 km in length. Many of these trackways are of the first millennium BC, and the variety in construction is extensive. Several are now known to have furnished a base for certain activities which can only be termed ritual. In the Ipfweger moor, for example, a wooden pathway of the third century BC had a series of wooden posts and at least two carved effigies set up beside the path (Hayen 1981) (figure 57). Other trackways are much more substantial, consisting of heavy planked roads suitable for sledges and wheeled vehicles (Hayen 1973; 1977; 1983). The conditions of preservation are variable, as is usual in peatbogs undergoing drainage and cutting for centuries, and some of the structures exhibit many of the carpentry techniques we normally associate with the production of more complex equipment such as wagons and boats.

An archaeological survey, to record the vanishing structures, has been under way for many years in the 700000 acres (280000 ha) of Lower Saxony peatbogs, and a large body of data has now been assembled. Tree-ring analyses and radiocarbon dating are extensively

Figure 56. A wooden road c. 1400 BC from Ipfweger Moor, Lower Saxony, Germany. This road is extremely heavy, and made of split logs laid transversely without need for edging or pegs, although longitudinal supports lie beneath the timbers. (Photo Schneider.)

Figure 57. Reconstruction of a wooden and turf-built trackway c. 3rd century BC from Ipfweger Moor. The wooden figures and other posts were found beside the track and are reconstructed here in their original setting. (From Hayen 1981.)

used. In addition to the trackways, many implements of wood, fragments of textiles, stone and metal artifacts, parts of carts and wheels used on the heavy roads, and 'bog bodies' have been found. The bog bodies are of the same general character as the famous Tollund and Grauballe men from the Danish bogs (Glob 1969), and some represent executions, criminal or sacrificial, of the late first millennium BC, although later bodies are also known. Held down in the bog on occasion, by stakes or hurdles, or lying free, clothed or unclothed, these bodies yield much information about Nordic physical types, diet, disease, and injuries, as well as clothing. At present, as the peatbogs are gradually worked out, and lower levels reached, it is only the wooden trackways which are under investigation, and time is certainly not on the side of the few archaeologists at work in the area. With such an abundance of evidence for local movements of people, the area is important as a guide to local communication in the Neolithic and later periods of human settlement in north Germany.

A closely comparable situation exists in the Somerset Levels in England, where a series of peatlands of 140000 acres (56000 ha) is being partly cut away for fertiliser and almost totally drained for agricultural purposes. In some parts, the original raised bog has been lowered by 6–8 m through cutting, with an additional shrinkage of the peat body by 0.5 m. Through field survey and excavation over the past 15 years, about 100 prehistoric trackways and platforms have been recorded, extending over c. 4000 years before the Roman conquest (Coles and Orme 1980). The trackways again range from heavy log-roads to slender bundle brushwood footpaths, and most were built to allow the former marshland to be crossed on foot. In times of flooding, water transport would have replaced trackways, and several logboats are known. The earliest structure is the Sweet Track, an Early Neolithic track 1800 m long, built of ash and oak planks with an elaborate substructure (figure 58). The archaeological work is closely related to tree-ring and environmental studies which allow close dating and precise wetland reconstruction (Morgan 1984; Caseldine 1984). The settlements of the Neolithic and Bronze Ages are out of the marsh, on the hills and islands, just as in north Germany. The contrast with the Fenland should be noted, for the Somerset Levels and Saxony moors were never dryland subsequently drowned. In the Later Iron Age, however, settlements became possible on the raised bog of the Levels

Figure 58. The Sweet Track, Somerset, England, c. 3700 BC at site SWWA. The roundwood rails, pegged by obliquely driven pegs and boards, provided a foundation for a plank walk; all of the planks at this site were dislodged by floodwaters and lie beside the rail base.

89

and Moors, and it is these which first attracted Bulleid to the area in the late nineteenth century. Their condition today is far from good.

A model of prehistoric and historic land-use patterns in such a wetland as Somerset explains why man was attracted to these areas. The combination of upland forests, well-drained slopes for agriculture, downslope meadowlands for grazing, and marshland wild produce would have been ideal for early settlers who had to establish a way of life reliant upon both wild and domesticated plants and animals. The Somerset Levels are now drying out, and archaeological survey must identify areas of interest for preservation or examination. In this work, many other agencies are active, with farming and nature conservancy as only two of the fundamental and traditional interests in the area. Just as in Lower Saxony, certain small pockets of peatbog have been designated for preservation, but these need adequate water supplies to prevent desiccation and the destruction of both archaeological and natural phenomena.

By wetlands is generally meant an area of former or current waterlogging, and by this definition we might include parts of urban sites where conditions have preserved that organic component normally absent on dry sites. The problems of urban wet archaeology are not much different from those of rural wetlands, and certainly no different from those of the prehistoric lakeside settlements of Alpine Europe.

At York, England, excavations of parts of the Viking city of Jorvik have encountered waterlogged deposits of great complexity and importance; deposits up to 6 m thick have yielded unique evidence about Viking and medieval urban life. In the major Coppergate area of the city, a row of tenth-century Viking tenements was uncovered; the buildings were made of oak timbers, and were separated by wattle fences. Within and around this site were vast quantities of waterlogged material, wood, leather, textile and bone, as well as inorganic materials relating to other crafts and activities. As important is the biological evidence for diet, health and disease, the study of which involves many specialists. Decisions regarding the conservation of this unique site are interesting to note here, as they include public involvement (Spriggs 1982). The rarity of these Viking structures, both in archaeological and technological terms, suggested that they should be preserved for future studies and for public display. Reconstructions, entirely modern, are often popular to the public, but rebuilding (at least in part) using genuine material is far more exciting and 'authentic'. The conservation of 1500 smaller artifacts also permit the Jorvik museum to be furnished with a unique display.

Broadly comparable circumstances existed in Viking and medieval Dublin, where waterlogged timber and wattle-and-daub houses of the tenth–thirteenth centuries were preserved in part, along with the organic and inorganic artifacts of the industries and market that existed in this favoured location. The deposits, 5–6 m deep in places, were particularly rich in the Wood Quay area where abutments onto the Liffey River were preserved. As in York, this was a unique opportunity to recover, record and preserve parts of the ancient town, but not all of the possibilities were fully explored. Similar opportunities have existed and been taken at other Viking or medieval towns in Europe, at Hedeby in north Germany, Novgorod in Russia, and for the Iron Age town at Biskupin in Poland.

In London, waterfront archaeology replaces wetland archaeology as the common descriptive term. Roman and medieval frontages on the River Thames have been well preserved by waterlogging, and exhibit unique evidence for timberwork and carpentry, as well as riverine traffic and trade. Excavations at Billingsgate, a trading station since Anglo-Saxon times, have also recovered vast quantities of wet materials of all sorts, and the study and conservation of these will take many years to complete (Keene 1982). These urban wet sites are not unique, and many ancient towns and cities, built on navigable rivers, have waterfronts and waterlogged deposits of great importance to our understanding of the origins and growth of urban centres.

Perhaps these urban centres are not true wetlands in our sense of the word, but they do encourage archaeologists to participate, and often lead, in the development of techniques which will allow a greater understanding of human behaviour in areas fortunate enough to contain waterlogged deposits.

Figure 59. Reconstruction of Neolithic settlement at Aichbühl, Federseemoor, Germany, based on studies in 1936. All of the houses, sheds, platforms, and boats are of wood or plant materials. (From Speck 1981; Schmidt 1930-37.)

A SUMMING-UP. The wetlands which have been intensively studied over past decades have yielded an abundance of evidence which could not be obtained from any other source. Though conditions of preservation are varied, the *yield* of information is immense, by comparison with dryland sites. Against this must be set the *cost* of wetland archaeology. All experience tells us that the expense of a wetland project will exceed that of a dryland enterprise by a factor of at least 3 and perhaps as much as 10. Yet, depending upon the wetland circumstances, the yield may outweigh even these factors. There is of course no conflict between a wetland and a dryland project. Each is important, and each will complement the other. For a settlement on a lakeside (figure 59), or a platform in a peatbog, or a crannog in a lake, will be fundamentally different from contemporary sites on a hill, or in a plain, or in a forest clearing. Wetland sites, therefore, cannot by themselves tell us about the whole range of human activities of the past. Wetland sites are not unusual, as the hundreds of lakeside occupations in the Alpine region clearly demonstrate, but they are not by any means the entire picture. Locational studies of these and other sites show the complementary nature of dryland and wetland settlement, but the point is often lost in the excitement of the yield from a wet site. The Neolithic settlements of Clairvaux and Chalain, in eastern France, are comprehensible only in relation to the whole landscape, which also contains several contemporary fortified stations in the Ain valley (CUER 1982). In the same way, the Iron Age occupations in the Somerset Levels did

92

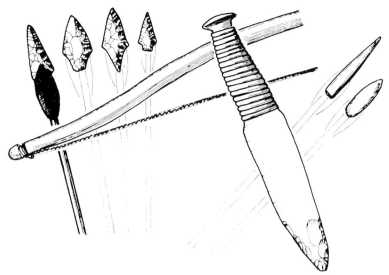

Figure 60. Artifacts from Neolithic settlements in the Alpine lakes, France, recovered by underwater archaeology. Some are composite flint, glue and wood, others are entirely of wood and other plant remains. (From CUER 1982.)

not exist in isolation, but formed part of a complex of human settlement and movement in and around the marshlands (Clarke 1972). Thus, to understand human behaviour patterns more fully we must take evidence from all sources, and both wetland and dryland sites will yield information relevant to the archaeological models which we use to try to explain how and why early societies acted as they did.

Dryland archaeology has been practised for decades, even centuries, and those archaeologists who rightly attempt to explain human behaviour have been largely restricted to using dryland evidence to build and test their models. We have seen above that dryland sites contain only – for the most part – imperishable materials, of stone, fired clay, and other inorganics, as well as bone on many occasions. These make up a small proportion of the material culture of almost every known society, extinct or living, and therefore it is axiomatic that behavioural models based on dryland sites are incomplete and biased.

Wetland sites are, equally, not perfect, and are variable in the type and quantity of evidence that has survived, but in general a waterlogged site will preserve a greater range of evidence than a dryland one. In attempting to explain past human actions, models that are

93

Figure 61. Carved cedar poles of west coastal Indian tribes, British Columbia, Canada. In dry land circumstances, such aspects of ancient cultures are almost totally absent or detectable only with great difficulty.

based on the evidence from wetland sites are going to be more complete, more accurate and more reliable. They will be based on fragments of events involving both organic and inorganic materials, and they are less biased towards any one or other material. Stone, flint and pottery assume their rightful place in the order, and are no longer the defining technologies or typologies for ancient societies that archaeologists often call 'cultures'. A society now represented by crude stone tools may have had a highly sophisticated industry in wood, more representative of its technical achievements (figure 60); the elaborate woodworking of the Indians of west coastal North America, involving totem poles, carved house fronts, large sea-going vessels and other decorated artifacts, reflects not only the technology but also the cosmology of the societies (figure 61). What would remain of such rich societies if all their organic materials had perished? We need only think of the wooden sculptured figures of the Late Iron Age from the source of the River Seine (Deyte 1983), or the beautiful jewel box,

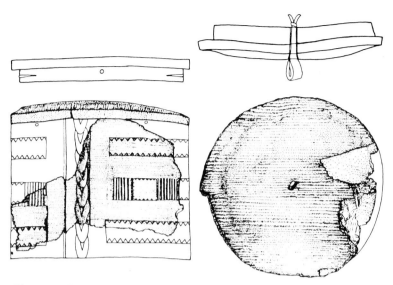

Figure 62. A wooden jewel box from the Late Bronze Age settlement at Grosser Hafnung, Zürich, Switzerland. Decorated by carving and with a lid held by woven material, it held a variety of glass beads and metal pendants. (From Wyss 1981.)

with its contents, from the Bronze Age of the Lake of Zürich (Wyss 1981) (figure 62), to realise that significant parts of the record will be missing without waterlogging, however caused. The preservation of 'offering places' for the deposition of warrior equipment in the first millennium AD at Illerup in Jutland, Denmark, promises to augment our very imperfect knowledge of such practices, not only through the yield of swords, spears and horse remains, but also through the precise details of the deposition sequence, preserved in the soft peats of the former marsh (Ilkjaer and Lønstrup 1983). In the same way, the discovery of a Bronze Age 'sanctuary' in the raised bog at Bargero-osterveld, Drenthe (figure 63), opens up new aspects of behaviour in the later second millennium BC (Waterbolk and van Zeist 1961).

The point probably needs no further argument, but one further example may be given; at the Ozette mudslide site in west coastal America, one of the prehistoric artifacts recovered was a massive cedar block carved into a whale dorsal fin, measuring c. $1 \times 0.5 \times 1$ m high, inlaid with over 700 seaotter teeth; the teeth were arranged in the design of a thunderbird holding a serpent in its talons, and the figures were painted in black on a red background (Inglis 1976). Archaeo-

95

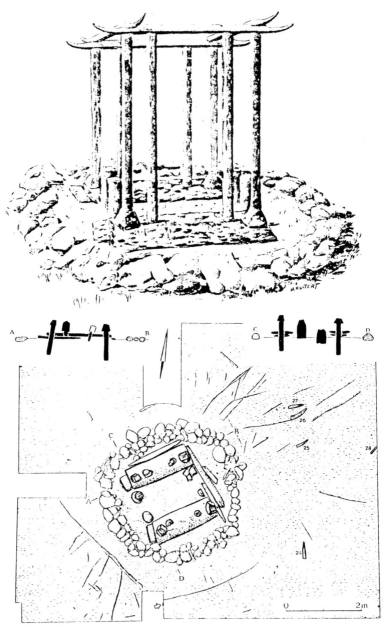

Figure 63. Plan (below), sections, and reconstruction (above) of the Bronze Age 'sanctuary' at Bargeroosterveld, Drenthe, showing the horizontal footings and bases of the uprights which formed the openwork structure. The fragments of carved and curved pieces (on the right of the plan) were interpreted as the horns of the uppermost timbers of the structure. (From Waterbolk and van Zeist 1961.)

logists who attempt to explain past human behaviour on the basis of evidence from dryland sites alone are in danger of ignoring, and perhaps ignorant of, a wealth of supplementary, corroborative or corrective information without which their models and theories are unnecessarily unreliable.

The argument has been advanced that wet sites offer a greater number of fossilised behaviour patterns than do the usual types of archaeological sites. A subsidiary point is that the inventory of organic artifacts, particularly those of wood or bark, are potentially capable of yielding greater insights into typological and technological developments than do stone or bone artifacts. We have many pottery typologies of great sophistication, which detail the changes in shape and design and provide chronological precision to our cultural groupings in various areas of the world, e.g. beakers of western Europe, Linearbandkeramik of central Europe, Iroquois pottery of the Great Lakes region in North America. The craftsmanship of wood, and particularly of basketry technology (figure 64) is even more sensitive to the preservation of small developmental changes which could aid the archaeologist (e.g. Bernick 1983; Croes 1976b). There is another prospect as well, although it may not be acknowledged by everyone: 'Moreover, and this aspect cannot be overemphasized, since a large proportion of the perishables from wet sites are baskets, mats, pouches, hats and so on, we obtain here concrete evidence of the important contributions that women made to prehistoric cultures on the Northwest Coast! Such evidence is often sorely lacking or difficult to discern in the impoverished archaeological assemblages from sites that contain only items of stone, bone, antler, and shell' (Borden 1976). The point is debatable, to say the least.

Of greater significance is the ability to identify clear use-patterns and functions in the organic artifacts from wet sites, among the digging sticks, ards, bows, boxes, baskets, textiles and bindings; in contrast, many assemblages of stone and bone from dryland sites contain entire classes of objects for which we have little or no idea of use, such as handaxes, burins, pounders, limpet-scoops, and carved stone balls. Only microwear studies and residues analysis could help here, and wetland deposition is sometimes necessary to preserve such traces.

The conservation of wetland artifacts, sites and landscapes must play a part in the discussion. Wetland artifacts once discovered will

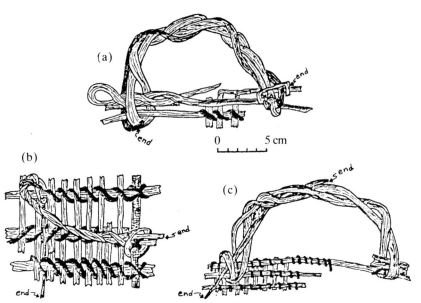

Figure 64. Detail of basketry handles from the Little Qualicum River, British Columbia, Canada. Such evidence provides details about the evolution of craftsmanship suitable for chronological purposes as well as the possible identification of individual hands. a) with twisted reinforcement through attachment loops; b) attached obliquely on outside of basket; c) inside view of open wrapped twining. (From Bernick 1983.)

deteriorate rapidly. They are needed for future studies of technology and to await the development of new techniques of analysis. They are needed to remind archaeologists of the importance which organic materials had in the life of ancient societies. And they are needed for public display and for the demonstration of ways of life which are more easily identifiable to the ordinary viewer.

Wetland sites must also be conserved if archaeology is to continue to develop new approaches to the study of ancient patterns of behaviour. Waterlogged sites are so rich in evidence of cultural and environmental factors that new techniques are needed to allow the information to be extracted and analysed. To allow known wetland sites to deteriorate through desiccation is to permit the evidence contained on the sites to be reduced by increasing factors with every year that passes. Fragile organic remains such as textiles, carved or painted details on wood, invertebrate animals and other susceptible remains disappear first, followed by more robust artifacts and evidence, until only inorganic

98

remains survive, and a dryland approach is appropriate. Postholes rather than posts, stone axeheads lacking their handles, flint arrowheads without shaft, feathering or bow, internal chronology of the site lost by decay of tree-ring evidence, all these are known losses. What cannot be even surmised will be the total absence of evidence for other actions, the identification of the individual craftsman or significant person, the artistic achievements, and the hints of religious or philosophical attitudes which are often represented by fragile and perishable artifacts.

Wetland sites cannot survive or be conserved outside their immediate environment, but neither can they be interpreted to the full if their contemporary landscape is lost (figure 65). The conservation of wetlands is a paramount requirement if archaeology hopes to build on the slender evidence already available. Archaeology is not the only subject interested in the preservation of wetlands, and nature conservation is a wide field in which archaeology must play a part if the unique opportunities already glimpsed through past endeavours are not to be wasted through inaction.

Figure 65. Aerial view of part of the Somerset Levels, England, a flattened raised bog now undergoing peat extraction (dark fields), and drainage for grassland pasture. Hidden beneath the peats are many prehistoric wooden structures of c. 3700-100 BC, including trackways, platforms, and settlements. The preservation of this archaeological evidence can only be achieved through collaboration with other wetland interests, particularly those concerned with nature conservation. (Photo J. Hancock.)

99

References

Andersen, S. (1980) Tybrind Vig: foreløbig meddelelse om en under-
søisk stenalderboplads ved Lillebaelt. *Antikvariske studier 4*,
7-22.

——(1983) En stenalderbåd fra Tybrind Vig. *Antikvariske studier 6*,
162-72.

Arnold, B. (1977) Les deux villages immergés du Bronze final
d'Auvernier: la station Brena et la station Nord. *Mitteilungsblatt
der Schweizerischen Gesellschaft für Ur- und Frühgeschichte
30/31*, 46-57.

——(1982) Cortaillod-Est: avec Icare et Neptune sur les traces d'un
village du Bronze final. *Archäologie der Schweiz 5*, 90-3.

——(1983) Les 24 maisons d'Auvernier-Nord (Bronze final). *Jahr-
buch der schweizerischen Gesellschaft für Ur- und Frühgeschichte
66*, 87-104.

Baddeley, A. D. (1971) Diver performance, in *Underwater Science: an
Introduction to Experiments by Divers* (eds J. D. Woods & J. N.
Lythgoe), 33-68. Oxford.

Bantelmann, A. (1975) *Die frühgeschichtliche Marschensiedlung beim
Elisenhof in Eiderstadt. Band 1*. Landschaftsgeschichte und
Baubefunde.

Bartholin, T. (1978) Alvastra pile dwelling: tree studies. The dating
and the landscape. *Fornvännen 73*, 213-19.

Baudais, D., P. Corboud & M-C. Nierlé (1982) L'occupation préhistorique de la baie de Corsier-Port GE. *Archäologie der
Schweiz 5*, 55-9.

Behre, K-E. (1976) *Die frühgeschichtliche Marschensiedlung beim
Elisenhof in Eiderstadt. Band 2*. Die Pflanzenreste.

Bernick, K. (1983) *A site catchment analysis of the Little Qualicum
River site, DiSc1: a wet site on the east coast of Vancouver Island,
B.C.* Mercury series *118*. Ottawa.

Bocquet, A. (1982) Les recherches archéologiques au lac de Paladru.
Histoire et Archéologie 64, 9-94.

Bocquet, A., M. Colardelle & R. Laurent (1976) Méthode de fouille
en lac ou en rivière. Prétirage, IX Congres UISPP, Nice.

Borden, C. (1976) A water-saturated site on the southern mainland coast of British Columbia, in Croes (1976), 233-60.

Bord na Móna (1981-2) *36th Annual Report.* Dublin.

Bulleid, A. & H. S. G. Gray (1911, 1917) *The Glastonbury Lake Village.* Glastonbury.

Capelle, T. (1983) Zur Produktion hölzerner Gefässe im vor- und frühgeschichtlichen Mittel- und Nordeuropa, in *Das Handwerk in vor- und frühgeschichtlichen Zeit* (eds H. Jankuhn, W. Janssen, R. Schmidt-Wiegand & H. Tiefenbach), 397-414. Göttingen.

Caseldine, A. E. (1984) Palaeobotanical investigations at the Sweet Track. *Somerset Levels Papers 10,* 65-78.

Caulfield, S. (1983) The Neolithic settlement of North Connaught, in *Landscape Archaeology in Ireland* (eds T. Reeves-Smyth & F. Hamond), 195-215. Brit. Archaeol. Rep. *116.*

Centre Universitaire d'Etude Régionales (1982) *Connaissance de la Franche-Comté. Villages Néolithiques des lacs du Jura.* Université de Franche-Comté, Besançon.

Clark, J. G. D. (1954) *Excavations at Star Carr.* Cambridge.

——(1963) Neolithic wooden bows from the Somerset Levels, England, and the prehistory of archery in north-west Europe. *Proc. Prehist. Soc. 29,* 50-98.

Clarke, D. L. (1972) A provisional model of an Iron Age society and its settlement system, in *Models in Archaeology* (ed. D. L. Clarke), 801-69. London.

Coles, J. M. (1976) The Somerset Levels: a concave landscape, in *Early Land Allotment* (eds H. C. Bowen & P. J. Fowler), 147-8. Brit. Archaeol. Rep. *48.*

Coles, J. M. & B. J. Orme (1980) *Prehistory of the Somerset Levels.* Somerset Levels Project.

Croes, D. R. (ed.) (1976a) *The excavation of water-saturated archaeo-logical sites (wet sites) on the northwest coast of North America.* Mercury series *50.* Ottawa.

——(1976b) An early wet site at the mouth of the Hoko River, the Hoko River site (45CA213), in Croes (1976a), 201-32.

Crowley, G. M. (1981) *The Late Quaternary environmental history of the Lake Bolac region of western Victoria, and its implications for aboriginal occupation.* Unpub. BSc thesis, Monash University.

CUER (1982). See Centre Universitaire (above).

Cushing, F. (1897) Exploration of ancient key-dweller remains on the Gulf coast of Florida. *Proc. American Philosophical Society 25* (153), 329-448.

Davidsen, K. (1983) Stenalderfund fra østersbankerved Kølholm i Roskilde Fjord. *Antikvariske studier 6,* 127-36.

Deyte, S. (1983) Les bois sculptés des sources de la Seine. *Gallia sup. 42,* CNRS, Paris.

Dowman, E. (1970) *Conservation in Field Archaeology.* London.

Egloff, M. (1977) Les fouilles d'Auvernier de 1971 à 1975. *Mitteilungsblatt der Schweizerischen Gesellschaft für Ur- und Frühgeschichte 30/31,* 2-4.

Egloff, M. (1981) Versunkene Dörfer der Urnenfelderzeit im Neuenburger See. *Archäologisches Korrespondenzblatt 11,* 55-63.

Eigner, J. (1978) Erfassung der Moore in Schleswig-Holstein aus der Sicht des Naturschutzes. *Telma 8,* 315-22. Hannover.

Evans, J. G. (1978) *An Introduction to Environmental Archaeology.* London.

Field, N. (n.d.) *Fiskerton in the Iron Age.* North Lincs Archaeol. Unit, Lincoln.

Furger, A. R., A. Orcell, W. E. Stöckli & P. J. Suter (1977) Die Ausgrabungen der neolithischen Ufersiedlungen von Twann (1974-1976). *Mitteilungsblatt der Schweizischen Gesellschaft für Ur- und Frühgeschichte 32,* 2-19.

Furger, A. R. *et al.* (1981) *Die neolithischen Ufersiedlungen von Twann.* Berne.

Geophysical Survey Systems (n.d.) *Radar Assessment of Peat Resources.* Hudson, NH.

Gilliland, M. S. (1975) *The Material Culture of Key Marco.* University of Florida.

Girling, M. A. (1984) Investigation of a second insect assemblage from the Sweet Track. *Somerset Levels Papers 10,* 79-91.

Glob, P. V. (1969) *The Bog People.* London.

Gleeson, P. & G. Grosso (1976) Ozette site, in Croes (1976a), 13-44.

Godwin, H. (1978) *Fenland: Its Ancient Past and Uncertain Future.* Cambridge.

———(1981) *The Archives of the Peat Bogs.* Cambridge.

Grattan, D. W. (ed.) (1982a) *Proceedings of the ICOM Waterlogged Wood Working Group Conference, Ottawa 1981.* ICOM, Ottawa.

———(1982b) A practical comparative study of several treatments for waterlogged wood. *Studies in Conservation 27,* 124-36.

Griffin, G. M. (1982) *Assessment of the Peat Resources of Florida, with a Detailed Survey of the Northern Everglades.* Governor's Energy Office, Florida.

Guyan, W. U. (1981) Zur Viehhaltung im Steinzeitdorf Thayngen-Weier II. *Archäologie der Schweiz 4*, 112-19.

Haarnagel, W. (1979) *Die Grabung Feddersen Wierde. Methode, Hausbau, Siedlungs- und Wirtschaftformen sowie Sozialstruktur.* Wiesbaden.

Hall, D. N. (1981) The Cambridgeshire Fenland: an intensive archaeological fieldwork survey, in *The Evolution of Marshland Landscapes* (ed. T. Rowley), 52-73. Oxford.

Hammond, R. F. (1981) *The Peatlands of Ireland.* An Foras Talúntais, Dublin.

Hayen, H. (1973) Rader und Wagen aus nordwestdeutschen Mooren. *Nachrichten aus Niedersachsens Urgeschichte 42*, 129-76.

——(1977) Der Bohlenweg VI (PR) im grossen Moor am Dümmer. *Materialhefte zur Ur- und Frühgeschichte Niedersachsens 15.*

——(1980) *Gedanken zum Schutz von Moor-Resten.* Holzberg, Oldenburg.

——(1981) *Moorarchäologie und Naturschutz.* Oldenburg.

——(1983) Handwerklich-technische Lösungen im vor- und frühgeschichtlichen Wagenbau, in *Das Handwerk in vor- und frühgeschichtlichen Zeit* (eds H. Jankuhn, W. Janssen, R. Schmidt-Wiegand & H. Tiefenbach), 415-70. Göttingen.

Heitz, A., S. Jacomet & H. Zoller (1981) Vegetation, Sammelwirtschaft und Ackerbau im Zürichseegebiet zur Zeit der neolithischen und spätbronzezeitlichen Ufersiedlungen. *Helvetica archaeologica 45-8*, 139-52.

Hinz, H. (ed.) (1980) *Bosau. Untersuchung einer Siedlungskammer in Ostholstein. IV. Naturwissenschaftliche Untersuchungen.* Offa-Bücher 42.

Hobler, P. (1976) Wet site archaeology at Kwatna, in Croes (1976a), 146-57.

Höneisen, M. (1982) Zurich-Mozartstrasse: ein neuentdeckter prähistorischer Siedlungsplatz. *Archäologie der Schweiz 5*, 60-5.

Ilkjaer, J. & J. Lønstrup (1983) Der Moorfund im Tal der Illerup-Å bei Skanderborg in Ostjütland (Dänemark). *Germania 61*, 95-116.

Inglis, R. (1976) Wet site distribution – the northern case GbTo33 – the Lachane site, in Croes (1976a), 158-85.

Johnson, F. (ed.) (1949) *The Boylston Street Fishweir II: a study of the geology, palaeobotany and biology of a site on Stuart Street in the Back Bay district of Boston, Massachusets.* Philips Academy, Andover, Mass.

Jørgensen, M. S. (1982) To jyske bronzealderveje – og en ny metode til arkaeologisk opmåling. *Nationalmuseets Arbejdsmark*, 142-52.

Keene, S. (1982) Waterlogged wood from the City of London, in Grattan (1982a), 177-80.

Keller, F. (1878) *The Lake Dwellings of Switzerland and Other Parts of Europe*. London.

Kinahan, G. H. (1897) Peat bogs and debacles. *Trans. Institution Civil Engineers of Ireland 26*, 98-123.

Lenihan, D. J. (ed.) (1981) *The Final Report of the National Reservoir Inundation Study*. US Dept of the Interior, Santa Fe.

Loy, T. (1983) Prehistoric blood residues: detection on tool surfaces and identification of species of origin. *Science 220*, 1269-71.

Luebbers, R. (1975) Ancient boomerangs discovered in South Australia. *Nature 253*, 39.

Lundstrom-Baudais, K. (1984) L'alimentation et les modes de cuisson au village néolithique de Charavines (Isère). *1er congrès internat. sur l'alimentation préhistorique et des sociétés primitives*. Les Eyzies.

Macdonald, G. (1982) The management of wet site archaeological resources, in Grattan (1982a), 123-8.

Macdonald, G. F. & B. A. Purdy (1982) Florida's wet sites: where the fragile past survives. *Early Man 4(4)*, 4-12.

Malmer, M. P. (1978) Forskningsprojeket Alvastra pålbyggnad. *Fornvännen 73*, 149-58.

Martin-Kilcher, S. (1979) Ferdinand Keller und die Entdeckung der Pfahlbauten. *Archäologie der Schweiz 2*, 3-11.

Morgan, R. A. (1984) Tree-ring studies in the Somerset Levels: the Sweet Track 1979-1982. *Somerset Levels Papers 10*, 46-64.

Morris, G. (1984) Microwear and organic residue studies on Sweet Track flints. *Somerset Levels Papers 10*, 97-106.

Morrison, A. (1980) Structures under water, in Muckelroy (1980), 156-61.

Muckelroy, K. (1978) *Maritime Archaeology*. Cambridge.

——(ed.) (1980) *Archaeology Under Water*. New York.

Mudge, W. (1836) Description of an ancient structure dug out of Drumkelin Bog, in the parish of Inver, county of Donegal, in the year 1833. *Archaeologia 26*, 361-7.

Müller-Beck, H. (1965) *Seeberg Burgäschisee-Süd. 5. Holzgeräte und Holzbearbeitung*. Acta Bernensia II.

Munsell, D. A. (1976) Excavation of the Conway wet site 45SK59b Conway, Washington, in Croes (1976a), 86-121.

Oddy, W. (ed.) (1975) *Problems of the Conservation of Waterlogged Wood.* Maritime Monographs *16.* Greenwich.

Orme, B. J. (1982) The use of radiocarbon dates from the Somerset Levels. *Somerset Levels Papers 8,* 9-25.

Orme, B. J. & J. M. Coles (1983) Prehistoric woodworking from the Somerset Levels: 1. timber. *Somerset Levels Papers 9,* 19-43.

Oshibkina, S. V. (1982) Wooden artifacts from the Mesolithic site of Nizhneye Veretye. *Archaeologické rozhledy 34,* 414-29.

Perini, R. (1976) Die Pfahlbauten im Torfmoor von Fiavè. *Mitteilungsblatt der Schweizerischen Gesellschaft für Ur- und Frühgeschichte 27,* 2-12.

———(1983) *Sulle tracce delle antiche genti giudicariesi.* Beni culturali nel Trentino. Trento.

Pétrequin, P. (1983) Etat actual des connaissances sur les problemès archéologiques. *Archives des Sciences (Genève) 36(2),* 215-32.

———(1984) *Gens de l'eau, gens de la terre.* Poitiers.

Pryor, F. (1983) South-west Fen-edge survey 1982/3: an interim report. *Northants Archaeology 18.*

Pryor, F. & I. Kinnes (1982) A waterlogged causewayed enclosure in the Cambridgeshire Fens. *Antiquity 56,* 124-6.

Purdy, B. A. (1982) Survey, recovery and treatment of wooden artifacts in Florida, in Grattan (1982a), 159-69.

Rackham, O. (1977) Neolithic woodland management in the Somerset Levels. *Somerset Levels Papers 3,* 65-71.

Ruoff, E. (1981) Stein- und bronzezeitliche Textilfunde aus dem Kanton Zürich. *Helvetia archaeologica 45-48,* 252-64.

Ruoff, U. (1981a) Die Ufersiedlungen an Zürich- und Griefensee. *Helvetia archaeologica 45-48,* 19-61.

———(1981b) Die Entwicklung der Unterwasserarchäologie im Kanton Zürich. *Helvetia archaeologica 45-48,* 62-70.

———(1981c) Alterbestimmung mit Hiife der Dendrochronologie. *Helvetia archaeologica 45-48,* 89-97.

———(1981d) Der 'Kleine Hafner' in Zürich. *Archäologie der Schweiz 4,* 2-14.

Salisbury, C. R. (1981) An Anglo-Saxon fish weir at Colwich, Nottinghamshire. *Trans. Thoroton Society of Nottinghamshire,* 26-36.

Schmidt, R. R. (1930-7) *Jungsteinzeit-Siedlungen im Federseemoor.* Augsburg.

Schweingruber, F. H. (1976) *Prähistorisches Holz.* Academica Helvetica 2.

——(1982) Conservation of waterlogged wood in Switzerland and Savoy, in Grattan (1982a), 99-106.

Sears, W. H. (1982) *Fort Center: an archaeological site in the Lake Okeechobee basin.* University of Florida.

Skaarup, J. (1983) Submarine stenalderbopladser i det sydfynske øhav. *Antikvariske studier 6,* 137-61.

Smith, Buckingham (1847) In *Everglades of Florida: acts, reports and other papers, state and national, relating to the Everglades of the State of Florida and their reclamation.* Senate Document *89,* 62nd Congress.

Speck, J. (1981) Pfahlbauten: Dichtung oder Wahrzeit? Ein Querschnitt durch 125 Jahre Forschungsgeschichte. *Helvetia archaeologica 45-48,* 98-138.

Spriggs, J. (1982) The conservation of timber structures at York – a progress report, in Grattan (1982a), 143-52.

Stephens, J. C. (1974) Subsidence of organic soils in the Florida Everglades – a review and update, in *Environments of South Florida: present and past* (ed. P. J. Gleeson), 352-61. Miami Geol. Soc. Mem. *2.*

Stotzer, M., F. H. Schweingruber, & M. Sebek (1976) Prähistorisches Holzhandwerk. *Mitteilungsblatt der Schweizerischen Gesellschaft für Ur- und Frühgeschichte 27,* 13-23.

Strahm, C. (1976) Deux stations lacustres sur le lac de Neuchâtel. *Archéologia 99,* 55-71.

Thesiger, W. (1964) *The Marsh Arabs.* London.

Thompson, M. (1967) *Novgorod the Great.* London.

Thorne, A. G. & P. G. Macumber (1972) Discoveries of Late Pleistocene man at Kow Swamp, Australia. *Nature 238,* 316-19.

Troels-Smith, J. (1981) Naturwissenschaftliche Beiträge zur Pfahlbauforschung. *Archäologie der Schweiz 4,* 98-111.

Warner, R. (1826) *A History of the Abbey of Glaston and of the Town of Glastonbury.*

Waterbolk, H. T. & W. van Zeist (1961) A Bronze Age sanctuary in the raised bog at Bargeroosterveld (Dr). *Helinium 1,* 5-19.

Williams, M. (1970) *The Draining of the Somerset Levels.* Cambridge.

Wyss, R. (1976) Das jungsteinzeitliche Jäger-Bauerndorf von Egolzwil 5 im Wauwilermoos. *Archaeologische Forschungen.*

—— (1981) Kostbare Perlenkette als Zeuge ältesten Fernhandels in Zürich. *Helvetia archaeologica 45-48,* 242-51.

106

Acknowledgements

Dr S. Andersen, Forhistorisk Institut, Moesgård, Aarhus, Denmark.
Prof. K. Behre, Niedersächsisches Landesinstitut für Marschen- und Wurtenforschung, Wilhelmshaven, Germany.
Ms K. Bernick, c/o Museum of Anthropology, University of British Columbia, Vancouver, Canada.
Dr J. Bill, Archaeologische Forschung im Fürtstentum Liechtenstein, Balzers.
Dr A. Boquet, Centre de documentation de la préhistoire alpine, Grenoble, France.
Dr J. Bouzek, Ústav pro klasickou archeologii, Prague, Czechoslovakia.
Canadian Wildlife Service, Ottawa.
Dr S. Caulfield, Department of Archaeology, University College, Dublin, Ireland.
Mr D. J. Clark, Victoria Archaeological Survey, Victoria, Australia.
Dr J. Eigner, Landesamt für Naturschutz und Landschaftspflege, Schleswig-Holstein, Kiel, Germany.
Prof. M. Egloff and Dr B. Arnold, Musée cantonal d'archéologie, Neuchâtel, Switzerland.
Dr D. Grattan, Canadian Conservation Institute, Ottawa, Canada
Dr G. M. Griffin, Department of Geology, University of Florida, USA.
Mr D. Hall, Fenland Survey, Department of Archaeology, University of Cambridge, England.
Mr J. Hancock, 26 Woodstock Road, Redland, Bristol, England.
Dr H. Hayen, Staatliches Museum für Naturkunde und Vorgeschichte, Oldenburg, Germany.
Dr P. Hoffmann, Stifung Deutsches Schiffahrtsmuseum, Bremerhaven, Germany
Dr V. Jenssen, Parks Canada, Ottawa, Canada.
Dr G. Macdonald, National Museum of Man, Ottawa, Canada
Miss B. J. Orme, Department of History and Archaeology, Exeter University, England.
Prof. R. Perini, Museo Provincial d'Arte, Trento, Italy.
Dr P. Pétrequin, CNRS, Gray, France.
Mr F. Pryor, Fenland Associates, Wisbech St Mary, Cambs, England.

Prof. B. Purdy, Department of Anthropology, University of Florida, Gainesville, Florida, USA.
Dr J. Reichstein, Landesamt für Vor- und Frühgeschichte von Schleswig-Holstein, Schleswig, Germany.
Mr M. Ryan, National Museum of Ireland, Dublin, Ireland.
Prof. M. Todd, Department of History and Archaeology, Exeter University, England.
Mme F. Vin, Centre de documentation de la préhistoire alpine, Grenoble, France.

Index

Fenland, 7, 24, 26, 28, 29, 82
Fiavè, 11, 18, 76, 77
field systems, 7, 52, 84, 85
fieldwork, 24, 28, 32
fishing, 13, 17, 20, 69, 71, 82
fish weirs, 12, 15
Fiskerton, 83
Flag Fen, 83
flies, 61
floating of deposits, 63
Florida, 3, 20, 27, 28, 34, 49, 52, 55, 78, 79
freeze-drying, 58
fungus, 63

Glastonbury, 11, 22, 23, 62
granulometric studies, 59
Grauballe, 88
Gray, H., 22
grids, 43ff

hafts, 20, 36, 58, 69, 71, 74
handles, see hafts
harpoon, 17
Hedeby, 91
Holme Fen, 27, 28
Hontoon, 49, 55
houses, 15, 22, 36, 54, 64, 73, 74, 75, 76, 81
humus, 59
hurdles, 16, 34, 36, 64, 74, 90, 91

identification of sites, 36
Illerup, 95
infra-red, 34
Ipfweger moor, 86, 87
Ireland, 4, 7, 32, 34, 52, 83, 84, 85

Keller, F., 19
Key Marco, 20, 53

Lachane, 26, 41, 42, 81
lakes, 2
lakeside sites, 17, 19, 20, 25, 32, 43, 44, 59, 63, 71, 73, 74, 76
landscapes, 69ff, 84ff
Lavagnone, 76
lifting, 54

Little Qualicum, 12, 40, 81, 82, 83
Little Salt Springs, 78
location of sites, 50
London, 91
looms, 22
Lower Saxony, 6, 25, 34, 35, 86

Manea, 29-31
marsh, 2
midden, 24, 25, 41, 54, 55, 81, 82, 90
molluscs, 61
Mörigen, 23
Morlot, A., 19
mudslide, 15, 24
muskeg, 8

Nizhneyo Veretye, 69, 70
Novgorod, 11, 56, 91

Okeechobee, 78
Ozette, 15, 40, 95

paddles, 20, 58, 71, 72, 81
paint, 71
Paladru, 43, see also Charavines
palisades, 20
pathways, see trackways
peat, 25, 62, 63, 78, see also peatbog
peatbog, 3, 8, 83
peat cutting, 25, 83, 86, 88
pH, 59
phosphates, 59
photographs, 50
plants, 2-3, 6-8, 12, 20, 54, 61, 62, 74
platforms, 12, 20, 35, 76, 78, 80, 83
pollen, 61, 62, 74
pollution, 41
polyethylene glycol, 56
polythene, 47, 48
pond, 2
post-excavation, 37
posts, 10, 17, 19, 32, 36, 44, 66, 76
preservation, 10, 11, 30, 38
pumps, 40, 44

quarrying, 24, 84

radar, 32